CATCH UP

HOW TO CATCH UP TO THE REST OF THE WORLD... IN 2 DAYS

WAYNE BUTCHER

Copyright © 2014 by Wayne Butcher
All rights reserved. This book or any portion thereof
may not be reproduced or used in any manner whatsoever
without the express written permission of the publisher
except for the use of brief quotations in a book review.

Printed in the United States of America

Book Cover Design by Vanessa Maynard (http://vanessanoheart.net)

First Printing, 2015

ISBN 978-1505570106

Catch Up
Sydney, Australia
www.catchupbook.com

Reader support requests:
support@catchupbook.com

For my friend Michael, a brave adopter

TABLE OF CONTENTS

FAST FORWARD 2 DAYS FROM NOW. WHERE ARE YOU?	1
CATCHING UP	7
WHO ARE YOU AND WHAT DO YOU DO?	15
"MAN, YOU'VE CHANGED."	23
YOUR NEW TOOLS OF TRADE	35
PROOF YOU CAN GET THIS DONE IN JUST 2 DAYS	39
AN MBA, $3 PER HOUR, EXCLUSIVELY YOURS, GO NUTS!	43
BEGIN BY OWNING YOUR DOMAIN	63
GETTING DIGITAL	75
IN THE CLOUD	93
COLLABORATION	109
YOUR DATABASE I	131
YOUR DATABASE II	141
SHARING DOCUMENTS	161
YOUR OWN WIKI	181
ACCOUNTING	193
YOUR WEB SITE I	205
SOCIAL MEDIA	239
YOUR NEW MARKETING MACHINE AT FULL SPEED	267
YOUR WEBSITE II	279
IN ACTION	285
JUST PUTTING IT OUT THERE	291
PERFECTING YOUR ACCOUNTING SYSTEM	299
A SCHEDULE FOR DELIVERING CONSISTENCY AND EXCELLENCE	305

1

FAST FORWARD 2 DAYS FROM NOW. WHERE ARE YOU?

"Three little tomatoes are walking down the road. Papa Tomato, Mama Tomato and Lil' Baby Tomato. Lil' Baby Tomato is going slow and laggin' behind and Papa Tomato gets all angry and goes back to Baby Tomato and squishes her and says "Ketchup!"

UMA THURMAN IN PULP FICTION

Dear courageous reader,

This is going to be a great ride!

Following this 2-day journey, you are going to be in a different place. You will feel a comfort and confidence that may not be with you right now. You will understand terms and concepts that previously provoked anxiety. You will be charged with a whole new energy that comes with new knowledge.

But with such liberty comes responsibility. You will be the champion in your organisation of a new way of doing things, a new way of communicating. You will have to carry the torch and show others that this new way of operating makes sense and that traversing the learning curve is worthwhile.

Because you have learned you will then have to teach. And, as with all learning, your thirst for more knowledge will help you to see more new ways and new possibilities for your business. This will truly feel like a new start.

But specifically, and in case you have to make a case for this new approach to others, here's what you will be armed with:

- You will be able to participate in the conversation with your business colleagues when the issue of the internet and social media and similar concepts come up. You will be up-to-date, current and aware.
- You will be able to understand, compete and know what others know.
- You will feel comfortable with new technology rather than afraid of it. In fact, you will get really excited by it – I promise you that!
- You will have personally (and quite easily) created a platform from which you can command the attention of your market. You will be online, known, vocal and, depending, how far you take this, famous!
- You will quickly emerge and be known as the authority in your field.
- You will be able to charge more.
- You will rekindle a sense of love for your customers because you will become an active and respected member of the commercial community that you serve.
- Your whole business will be online, mobile and secure. You could come, go, scale down or grow as you please
- Your admin costs will be reduced by approximately 48%
- You will be largely paper-free
- You will control your web presence (and be proud of it)
- You will have 24/7, global access to ever single bit of data within your business. You will be 'In The Cloud'

... and loving it up there!
- Your debtor cycle will be about 11 days.
- You will have accurate and immediate access to your financial accounts.
- Your staff will stay longer, work harder and enjoy it because they want to work for a market leader, a business that is current.

Whilst all of these benefits will get delivered when you install the practices that this book deals with, there is something much more important at stake. It's the promise that this book will enable you to make to your customers.

Consider that when you first interact with your clients, before they've made a decision to buy, they are full of two things: (1) expectations; and (2) fears.

They expect to get what they need but they are also afraid that they won't.

What this book enables you to do is to *promise* that their expectations will be met and that none of their fears will be realised.

In fact, following your completion of the work in this book, I encourage you (strongly) to make a written promise to each one of your customers that sounds something like this:

"We guarantee that if you do not receive the value you were expecting from us, you do not have to pay our bill."

If you do happen to complete all of the work in this book, I personally guarantee that you will be able to make that promise to every one of your customers and never have to return a single penny.

Let me show you how to do that …

2

CATCHING UP

THE SUMMARY ON WHAT HAS BEEN HAPPENING IN THE REST OF THE WORLD WHILE YOU'VE BEEN FIXING YOUR FAX MACHINE

"Procrastination is the art of keeping up with yesterday"

DON MARQUIS, AMERICAN NOVELIST

In this book you're going to discover just how close you are (and have been for a while) to an amazing array of people, applications and tools that will make your business and working life much easier.

Let me explain a few of the things that have occurred in the last few years that have created a wellspring of new technology that is now available online.

CASH

It's a gold rush! Just like people ran to the hills when gold discoveries were on, people are running as fast as their internet will carry them in the same direction as Mark Zuckerberg (Facebook), Max Levchin (PayPal) and Larry Page (Google) because that's where the cash is.

As this flight towards online continues, you the user are the beneficiary. All of this development is for you. Budding online entrepreneurs are pulling all-nighters, maxing out their credit cards, borrowing from friends and families or raising millions of speculative dollars just to bring you the latest in a stream of online creations designed to make your life easier, better, wealthier, happier, …

Some would have you believe that you ought to be gold panning out there with the rest of them. No. Your best position is not out there. It's exactly where you are, doing what you're best at and using everything that is being created to help you become better and wealthier and happier thanks to all of this innovation that is being created for you.

Of course, you do have a choice. You can maintain the status quo, rely on what you know. Or, you could evolve. Take your current business model and make the most of the incredible innovation that is being laid out before you. This is what 'Catch Up' is all about.

A FLAT WORLD

"Global Outsourcing" has become a catch-cry. it is used so often. But beneath this phrase is one of the world's most important revolutions. Except for where physical presence is essential to completing a task, any task can now be performed by anyone able to do it, in any country, at any time and for any amount. That is a miracle!

Many books have been written about this phenomenon and many commentators have developed strong opinions about it. The best book and author that I know of, a guy that shaped some of my earliest opinions about this, is a guy call Thomas Friedman. He wrote a book called *The World Is Flat*. Read it. It's incredible.

Consider for a moment that you run an architecture firm. Unless you have an enormous firm, your workload and revenue would best be described as a bit lumpy. Big job >> furious pace >> no work >> big job >> furious pace >> no work. This cycle has a number of side-effects. One of the worst of which has to be the staffing, doesn't it? Unless you can provide your team with a continuous stream of new work you will most likely suffer some incredibly costly idle time.

Or let's say you run an accounting firm. You make money from the 'providing advice' part of the business but the bookkeeping side is just a non-profitable chore. So then what?

Well, in both of these situations, a flexible workforce is the answer. Flexible not just in terms of working when the work appears but also flexible in terms of cost.

So when the architect needs an engineer, what does she do? Or when the accountant needs to provide the unprofitable bookkeeping service, what does he do?

Both of them can access an enormous, international, highly skilled pool of talent that exist online and are available on-call, whenever the need arises. The architect gets her engineer as and when the need arises and she retires the engineer at the completion of the project only to bring them back when the need arises. The accountant still provides the bookkeeping service but outsources it to someone offshore who will do it well and cheaply and still enable the accountant to deliver the service under their brand.

If you haven't explored this pool of talent yet, you have overlooked one of the most compelling arguments for starting a business today and one of the most profitable ways of running a business. Previously, one of the reasons that you would NOT start a business was because the fixed costs were frightening. A very large part of fixed costs is wages and the people aren't negotiable about when or if they get paid. However, drawing upon a pool of talent that are available online from around the world is a brilliant solution.

We talk more about this in Chapter 7. We show you where they are and we also show some examples of what is possible by using these people to get your work done.

A TRULY WORLD-WIDE MARKET

The boom in online business is not necessarily because each person is suddenly spending more. It's because you can now access more people who are spending. Online businesses truly cater to a world-wide market. Even the tiniest niche can be profitable when you consider how many people belong to it around the world. You'll be interested to see just how many people you can reach with your existing products when you get your business online and open to the world.

In the next chapter we talk about how to refine your niche ... and own it!

14 CATCH UP

3

WHO ARE YOU AND WHAT DO YOU DO?

THE ARGUMENT FOR DEFINING AND SUPER-NICHING.

Right there in your driveway, is a really fast car. Not one of those stupid Hamptons-style, rich-guy, showy cars like a Ferrari, but an honest fast car, perhaps a Subaru WRX. And here are the keys. Now go drive it. Right there, on the runway, is a private jet, ready to fly you wherever you want to go. Here's the pilot, standing by. Go. Leave. Here's a keyboard, connected to the entire world. Here's a publishing platform you can use to interact with just about anyone, just about anytime, for free. You wanted a level paying field, one where you have just as good a shot as anyone else? Here it is. Do the work

SETH GODIN IN THE FOREWORD TO STEVEN PRESSFIELD'S
'DO THE WORK'

16 CATCH UP

The quote above talks about something really powerful. Whilst it is meant as a shot in the arm for budding creatives and entrepreneurs, it also contemplates that our access to technology allows us to immediately walk out on a stage and speak to a worldwide audience.

However, the other side to this immense opportunity is – so can anyone else. There's a lot of people out there. Lot of noise! So how do you cut through?

SUPER-NICHING

Well, I think the answer is buried in something that a smart friend of mine explained to me. His name is Gerard. Gerard explained the concept of super-niching. It's quite simple really – you take a niche and you super-size it, backwards. You make it smaller, more niche, more defined.

Let's take a simple example – a law firm. What does your local law firm do? They practice law. Hmmm … that's not terribly unique.

You know Google, yes? And you also know that the best position on Google is on the front page, right? Of course. Let's take it a step further – you know that to get to the front page of Google takes one or both of the following things:

skill and money.

So, with that said, and knowing that Google literally searches hundreds of billions of websites, do you reckon there's a fair chance that a big pile of these billions of sites relate to 'law'?

Now, what about Environmental Law in Connecticut? Still a few but far fewer, yes? That's a niche. In fact, it's a 'super-niche'. The potential exists to dominate that niche. The dominant player in any niche gets to control the terms upon which they conduct business. However, operating in a large sector, the opposite of a niche, has a whole different set of market forces which typically lead to two things – regulation and price competition, ie lower profits.

This simple Google example shows the importance of *super-niching* in business. Plus, the strategies that you will implement in the next 2 days will allow you to own the niches that you operate in, quickly. That's difficult to do in broad market categories.

Another reason you want to be in a super niche is so that you can be the best in the market at something. Other benefits that we discuss include – keywords become easier, you know where your market is, you know what they're interested in, you know what to talk to them about and you know what you need to do to satisfy them.

When it comes to making videos, using social media, building a website, writing a blog (all of which you will be able to do in just minutes) you will know exactly what the content needs to be and it will all be laser-focussed on your ideal clients.

Whilst concepts like *super-niching* may seem like a departure from the essence of what you are in business to do, understand that as important as your skill in your profession is, marketing is much more important to the success of your business. From now on, you are in marketing first and [your profession] second.

DEFINING

Operating in a super-niche starts with one activity – defining the niche. Defining the niche involves two things:

(1) Defining the profile of the typical customer – or, if you like, the common problem that they all come to you with.

(2) Defining the set of work that you do – how you solve the problem they come to you with.

FOR EXAMPLE:

Gary's Green Plumbing Service

"Our customers are all from the northern metropolitan areas around Cincinnati, Ohio and they call us when they have problems with their green plumbing systems. We are specialists in the area of 'green' plumbing systems including rainwater tanks and grey-water garden irrigation systems"

Boom! Gary owns that space. Now, how hard do you think it would be for Gary to broadcast a message about his business and get the attention of exactly the audience that he is after? Not too hard. On the other hand, how much energy do you think Gary would need to exert to make a discernible noise amongst all the other general plumbers in Ohio clambering for business … ?

Carry this concept with you on this journey. There is a very strong argument for super-niching your business and it starts with a clear definition.

When you can define your business through the narrow channel of a super-niche it becomes so much easier to see who the customers are, where they live, what they want, what they read and, importantly, how you can get their attention.

While we are focussed on the customer, let's have a look at what's been going on for them recently ...

4

"MAN, YOU'VE CHANGED."

WHAT TECHNOLOGY HAS DONE TO YOUR CLIENTS' EXPECTATIONS

The golden rule for every business man is this:
Put yourself in your customer's place

ORISON SWETT MARDEN, AMERICAN WRITER
AND HOTEL OWNER

What an exciting time to be in business!

New technology has levelled out the playing field. With all of the new tools, new ways of communicating and new methods of marketing, it's as though commerce has been reset to give everyone the same chance as each other.

Whether you've been in business for ten years or for ten minutes, your access to new technology is the same. It's online, it's available around the world and it's mostly free! Your decision whether or not to embrace it is one of the main things that will determine how competitive you are.

While you decide, know that your customers have already decided. They are voting unanimously in favour of the new technology and those businesses that adopt it.

You can't do business on the phone with someone who wants to do business online. You can't send a fax to someone who doesn't have a fax machine. You can't respond to a tweet if you're not on Twitter. You have to take your business to the market. You have to go where the market is. Today, the market is online. Let's go there …

You'll see in Chapter 17 that being 'online' is far more than just having a website. Being 'online' means that you have these elements as a part of your operation:

- You can talk with your market across a wide range of communications platforms. Not just the phone or email
- You can operate from anywhere and others can collaborate with you wherever they are
- Your data and your clients' data is stored securely in the 'Cloud' and accessible 24/7
- You are transparent and visible to your clients
- Your staff have access to technology that makes their work easier and more efficient
- Your operation is scalable, quickly

The extent to which your business has all of these elements you are an eligible contender for new business. To the extent that some of them are missing, you risk being considered out-of-date.

Let's have a look at some of these features in real-life business scenarios:

THE 'NEW' BUSINESS:

Customers want to know that the businesses they choose to work with are authorities in their field. As you will read several times in this book, your ability to become an authority on your subject is given by the extent to which you talk about what you do.

Communications – everything but the phone

These days, everyone has access to a free, international publishing platform – the internet. You can tweet, post on Facebook, create your own videos for YouTube and even broadcast live from your computer in a webinar. If you put two professionals next to each other from the same industry with the same experience, even working at the same firm, the one that adopts these new communications tools most assertively will almost always appear as the authority in their field.

All professionals have an amazing opportunity to demonstrate their skill and knowledge by distributing their message across this platform. As more clients and prospects scan these tools while they are deciding who to work with, those who aren't appearing on them are quickly going to become irrelevant.

Work anywhere, with anyone

Imagine you have a client who travels. You have two options – you can wait until he comes back to the country before you have your next meaningful exchange with him. Or, you can get online and chat with him on Skype.

Consider also that you have a client that is made up of several people. For example, your client is a company with 7 people on a project team. You could send 7 emails every time you want to update the team or you could post each update to a website that all 7 of them have access to and they can get their updates as they choose to. Chapter 11 will show you a tool that does this brilliantly.

Perhaps you have a client that is in a different time zone to you. You could wait at the office to receive her emails at odd hours or you could use a Cloud-based email service that allows you to access emails at any hour, wherever you are.

If you don't use the latest technology tools for communicating, your staff will most likely have to be within eyesight. You will not be able to work with others who may be off-site or even off-shore.

If your clients see that you don't have the mobility and flexibility that is enabled by being online, you may just become too hard to work with.

Is my data safe and accessible?

If you're a lawyer, an accountant or any other business dealing with sensitive, valuable data, you will eventually have to let your clients know how you manage their data. To say that it is in hard copy format at your premises will be unlikely to impress those clients who have learned that the safest way to keep their data is to store it in the Cloud where it is not subject to fire, floods or being misplaced.

Few clients are likely to accept they can't see their data whenever they want it and fewer still are going to be happy about having to call you every time they need information.

You are eventually going have to find a way to store their data safely and allow them access to it as they please.

About Us

Being 'online' means adopting an approach to business which is entirely different to the way business has been conducted in the past.

'About Us' used to be a couple of paragraphs about your business and a nice photo of the owner.

Now, 'About Us' is an invitation to explore every nook and cranny of the organisation – here's us on Twitter, find us on Facebook, check out the photos of us at our Christmas party on Flickr, subscribe to our weekly newsletters – a complete opening for the public to get to know you.

This is only possible, mind you, by using the tools that we discuss in this book. But please note, these conditions don't exist because we wrote this book. We wrote this book in response to the emergence of these conditions. This book will enable you and your business to navigate your way through these conditions with ease and confidence. That will place you in an enviable position in your market – knowledgeable and current.

Give them the best tools

Your team, whether large or small, are a lot like your clients – quickly becoming more informed about new technology. Therefore, they too will start to expect more from you.

One of the main benefits of embracing the approach to business that we promote is not just that you'll meet and exceed your clients' expectations but that you will capture the attention and interest of your staff.

It's not terribly inspiring to work for a business that is outdated. In contrast, the output of your team (even if it is just you) will be a lot higher and you will find it easier to attract and keep the best talent when you provide your team with the best, most relevant tools for their job.

Also, your team members are most likely using some of these tools as part of their own private life's activities. They are almost definitely on Facebook, they may have their own Twitter account, they are probably already used to the Gmail interface so they are all very comfortable with being online. Use this to your advantage. Make them the champions of your bold move online. Get them to own parts of the adoption program. Let them help you by getting everyone enrolled. Get their help in using your new tools. This is one of the best things you can do to their level of engagement.

We need it yesterday!

Your clients will never order when you need them to. In fact, they will usually order all at the same time and then they'll leave you alone for too long.

They have no insight or regard for your productive capacity or for your convenience. They just want the advice, the report, the designs or the information yesterday!

And, of course, you wish to oblige. Thankfully, your new resources will allow you to. You will have access to offshore temporary staff, all of your software is expandable and contractible at a moment's notice and, however you choose to handle things, your appearance to anyone on the outside is truly larger than life thanks to the way your brand is spread all over your niche.

Your clients expect you to be able to pivot on a dime, turn things around overnight, grow and shrink according to their needs and now you can!

Now, stay with me. I'm going to show you a system that makes all of this a reality. And far from being 'hard work', it will be a big part of the energy and excitement within you and your whole team. Just watch. We'll show you *exactly* how to do it. Because in the next section you'll see all of the incredible tools that you'll learn to use and exactly what benefit they will deliver to you and to your clients and to your team ...

5

YOUR NEW TOOLS OF TRADE

(AND THEY'RE MOSTLY FREE)

A determined soul will do more with a rusty monkey wrench than a loafer will accomplish with all the tools in a machine shop.

ROBERT HUGHES, AUTHOR

Today one of the most frustrating things is the infinite choice of tools for business. The amount of information that one needs to process in order to arrive at a confident decision about what to use is so large that most choose not to choose.

Instead, what if you had a friend who knew all of the tools, knew how they worked and had actually used them with great results and was going to sit with you for two days and show you exactly how to install them and how to make the most of them?

Well, that's the purpose of this book. After years of trial and several errors we have seen just about every tool out there for business and we have created a brilliant system that businesses can use to get a major advantage in the area of customer service and business operations.

We'll sit with you and guide you through the installation process. We are sure that you'll be very pleased with the results!

Let me introduce you to our favourite tools for business. Below there is a list of the programs that we are about to place within your toolkit.

GOOGLE APPS FOR WORK
GOOGLE DRIVE
GOOGLE SITES
GOOGLE CALENDAR
GOOGLE ANALYTICS
GOOGLE MY BUSINESS (PLACES)
DROPBOX
FRESHBOOKS
XERO
BASECAMP
HIGHRISE
WIKISPACES
WORDPRESS
MAILCHIMP
ELANCE, GURU AND ODESK
FACEBOOK
TWITTER
YOUTUBE

Apart from a couple of the titles above, you would have heard of most of these programs. You have almost certainly used some of them. But let me make a point – it's not just using them that makes a difference to your business. It's how you use them and knowing how to use them well. That's what this book is all about.

6

PROOF YOU CAN GET THIS DONE IN JUST 2 DAYS

We are currently not planning on
conquering the world

SERGEY BRIN, CO-FOUNDER, GOOGLE

You can take the title of the book seriously – Catch Up ... In 2 Days. It's entirely possible. We've tested it.

Anything that takes more than two days is a fully-blown project. 2 days can happen in the space of a weekend, it's a short break. It's a task.

We really want you to get it done quickly and move on. Set it up fast and adjust it often. Like any good start-upper will tell you – ship the product then fix it.

You will build this platform and then discover all the amazing things that it enables but it's not until you've built it that you'll understand the power it will give you. It's then that your motivation will peak and provide the energy to refine it, improve it and continue its development.

So build it in faith, knowing that you are creating something powerful from which you and your business will draw a major commercial advantage.

Here's how it's possible. Below you'll see your schedule. It shows how long each section takes. Once you're familiar with this move on to the next chapter where you'll see exactly how the process works.

DAY 1	CATCH UP
9.00AM	HIRE YOUR VA
10.00AM	
11.00AM	CAPTURE YOUR DOMAIN
12.00PM	DIGITISE YOUR DATA
1.00PM	LUNCH BREAK
2.00PM	SET UP YOUR CLOUD-BASED EMAILS
3.00PM	INSTALL BASECAMP
4.00PM	
5.00PM	INSTALL HIGHRISE
6.00PM	OVERTIME - ANYTHING YOU MAY HAVE MISSED

DAY 2	CATCH UP
9.00AM	INSTALL MAILCHIMP
10.00AM	
11.00AM	INSTALL DROPBOX AND GOOGLE APPS
12.00PM	
1.00PM	LUNCH BREAK
2.00PM	INSTALL YOUR WIKI
3.00PM	INSTALL FRESHBOOKS & XERO
4.00PM	SET UP YOUR WEB PRESENCE
5.00PM	COMMENCE YOUR SOCIAL MEDIA CAMPAIGN
6.00PM	POPULATE! ADD DATA TO YOUR NEW PROGRAMS

If you think this looks reasonable and you're prepared to invest a couple of days to become a business champion, then read on ...

7

AN MBA, $3 PER HOUR, EXCLUSIVELY YOURS, GO NUTS!

By 'flat' I did not mean that the world is getting equal. I said that more people in more places can now compete, connect and collaborate with equal power and equal tools than ever before. That's why an Indian in Bangalore can take care of the office work of American doctors or read the X-rays of German hospitals.

THOMAS FRIEDMAN, AUTHOR – THE WORLD IS FLAT

For some readers, this book will indulge their curious spirits and that is all. It will be a pleasant read and will fuel an interesting debate at the office the following day. Others will read it, enjoy it, pick from it those tips that work for them and leave the rest for later, or never. However, for most readers, this book will be a tool that is used as a transformational weapon. It will mark the turning point for them and their business and it will spark a thirst for further, continual learning about this fascinating new world of business. Every reader is a friend and all are welcome. But for those who are up for the challenge, your time starts as you start this chapter. Your 2 days starts now …

From here on, you will notice the Activities at the end of each chapter. These are the steps showing exactly what to work on as you progress through this book.

Should you choose to accept the 2-day challenge, you can perform these Activites and literally transform your business upon any given 2-day period. Perhaps next weekend … ?

For anyone who is doing the 2-day challenge, we encourage you to get access to the Workbook that goes along with this book. The Workbook accompanies you throughout your two days and shows you step-by-step how to complete all of the Activities discussed in this book. It's not mandatory. You can still make a big difference without it but the Workbook is a very helpful addition to this book.

GET THE WORKBOOK NOW

Go to: www.catchupbook.com

For anyone who purchases the Workbook and takes on the 2-day challenge, we encourage you to join our community for support throughout your 2-day project. You will have access to a support team who have done this successfully in the past and who know all about it.

Simply send an email to: support@catchupbook.com and we'll provide any support you need throughout your journey.

In the next section we are going to introduce you to your new off-site workforce that are going to do most of the hard work for you. Come and meet the team that is going to instantly turn you from a jack-of-everything into a focussed, discerning entrepreneur ...

OUTSOURCING – MAKING EVEN THE SMALLEST BUSINESS ACT BIG

I know you've heard about outsourcing. It's a buzz-word. It seems that everyone is doing it, or wants to. But apart from getting your kid brother to design your logo, what does outsourcing mean and how can it help me?

All is about to be revealed …

Your service/product is more than just your service/product. It's the total aggregate of several inputs. For example – you're a plumber. Let's also say that you're a sole operator. So you are probably sending out invoices to clients that include an amount for your time and the cost of parts used in each job.

Any money you receive is really compensation for not only fixing a leaking tap but it is also compensation for the time that you spend preparing invoices, chasing cash, advertising, managing the administrative parts of your business and all the other things that go along with being in business for yourself. If you could reduce the cost and the time required for each input that goes into delivering the service/product, you would instantly become more profitable.

Let's choose one of the most time-consuming examples to illustrate something here – invoicing. I mean, for a small business, surely one of the most painful things about running the business has to be preparing the invoices, sending them out and, on top of it all, making sure they get paid!

The amount of time people spend on this task alone, in almost every business, is frightening. In the case of the plumber, an hour on-site can easily translate to double that in chasing bad payers. Plus, the most frustrating thing of all is the fact that these activities require exactly none of your professional skill and add zero value to your business. They are pure and simple admin and, unless you're into this sort of thing, they just plain suck!

Further, if our friend Peter the plumber is spending all his time on stupid admin, three things happen -

1. He is able to spend less time on his business doing work that actually pays the bills.
2. He spends his days plumbing and his nights doing the darn paperwork!
3. His business eventually becomes less competitive because he is spending all his time on paperwork and then his prices inevitably go up to compensate.

What if there was a way to effectively and very efficiently allow our friend Peter to get back to what he does best and leave someone else to handle all of the admin? There is.

What we are going to talk about here is the single most

important industrial shift in our lifetime. It's a ripple that is quickly becoming a huge wave. It's a wave that could either wipe out your business or, if you learn how to surf it, could turn into the ride of your life!

It's easy to disregard countries like India, Romania and the Philippines when you think about your business. It's easy to assume that whatever is happening in those countries is completely irrelevant to whatever is happening in your business. I mean, what do they know about Peter's plumbing business in Canada?! Well, they may not know a lot about plumbing in Canada, but don't think they can't learn and don't think they won't.

The internet is the greatest democracy in the world. It's available to almost everyone, almost everywhere and almost for free. In this incredible democracy, the people are free to do whatever they choose and to use the medium however they choose. Some people choose to use it for emails and Facebook. For others it's a powerful business tool and for many it's their primary means of education.

Most of the folks in these countries that you rarely think of are studying. They are using the internet to help them access information from around the world and they are very quickly becoming more educated and more capable than anyone else. The country borders that used to prevent them from threatening local industry do not apply in this new democracy. They are free to enter our territory and completely alter the way we do business and the terms upon which we do it.

Let's go back to our friend Peter. How on earth does Peter and his little plumbing business get help from a guy called Maneesh who lives in a town that has no plumbing?! Well, Maneesh may not even have running water but he's got the internet and, you know what? He's got a bachelor's degree as well.

Can you remember what the bane of Peter's business life was? That's right – the paperwork. Well, guess what Maneesh loves more than anything else? That's right – the paperwork. The internet has facilitated Maneesh's education and now it brings him and his skills to your doorstep. He's here. He's now a part of your local workforce. His rates are ridiculously low, he's the most committed employee you've ever heard of and he's either going to work for you or your competitor and, either way, bring extraordinary efficiencies to whichever business he works for.

There's something unique about a business owner – they value time in a very different way than someone who is being paid for their time regardless of how well they perform. All of your new 'employees' are going to be business people in their own right. Even though their business may be an old laptop on top of a desk the size of a postage stamp in the middle of a third world war zone, they are every bit as proud of their commercial stake in the ground as you are about yours.

They care about their brand and their reputation and they need to still be in business tomorrow for the same reasons you do – breakfast, lunch, dinner and a roof over their head. No wonder then that you will get service with a smile from your new team members. You are likely to be their best client!

HOW CAN PETER WORK WITH MANEESH?

Where do I find him?

If you decide to make the most of the incredible pool of highly skilled international talent out there, you will not be the first. Those before you have put a lot of thought into how to connect you with the thousands of professionals out there that are eager to find you and work for you. All of the following websites are portals that allow these professionals to post a profile that includes their resume, their portfolio of work and a list of reviews from previous employers.

- elance.com
- guru.com
- odesk.com

As an employer, you can create your own profile and then post job ads to the attention of thousands of people from all over the world. Plus, these services are entirely free to join!

WHAT CAN THESE PEOPLE DO?

In short, these people can do anything that doesn't require a physical presence. In this talent pool you will find everyone from Architects, Engineers and Lawyers through to data entry clerks.

HOW MUCH DO THEY COST?

Their rates vary depending on (1) where they are; (2) what they do; and (3) how good they are. However, as an indication, you can hire a degree-qualified marketing assistant based in the Philippines who knows all about the internet, websites and online marketing for US$400 per month. For a typical 40-hour week that equates to $2.31 per hour.

There is no sick pay, no maternity leave, no 401k or superannuation payments, no VAT, GST or sales tax. Just the most enthusiastic, devoted employee you've ever had the pleasure of working with.

Now, before you cry 'extortion', your $2.31 is about 30% more than they're getting locally and you're probably going to provide them with the opportunity to work from home rather than commuting for hours each day to an office in a distant town, away from their family. Far from being an oppressor, you will be their hero!

WHO SHOULD I HIRE?

You are going to start with two new employees:

1. A Virtual Assistant; and
2. A Bookkeeper

WHAT'S A VIRTUAL ASSISTANT?

In simple terms – it's a personal assistant, at a distance. As a business owner, you are in one of two categories: (1) you have an assistant; or (2) you want one.

Let's say you don't have one, think about the joy your life would become if you had one. Someone to answer your phone, someone to respond to your email, someone to do everything that you hate doing ... oh, the joy.

Well, joy, yes but also – diligent entrepreneur. In one of the most influential business books of all time, The E-Myth, Michael Gerber writes about the difference between the entrepreneur and the technician. His book encourages entrepreneurs to embrace again their very first notions of business – the enactment of a grand vision. To again become inventors, possessed by a powerful mission. He argues that most business owners become quickly burdened by the tedium of business – the admin, the invoicing, the staff problems. They lose sight of what they created the business for because they don't have time or the mental condition to dream their business anew, daily. Which is what he says is the key to good business – to every day make your business new again. Tall order it would seem for Peter the Plumber who still can't get the February invoices paid!

But Gerber's vision for the entrepreneur as a dreamer and a visionary comes to life again when you're working with Maneesh. My friends, Maneesh is going to set you free!

If you have a personal assistant, that is wonderful and you don't need to get rid of them, just yet. However, if you don't have one I can bet that there are two reasons: (1) you can't afford one; and (2) you wouldn't really know what to have them do anyway.

Well, at $400 per month, you'll see shortly that you can't possibly afford to be without one and in the previous chapter you just saw all the work ahead. My best suggestion is that you don't try to tackle it all yourself. You're going to do well with some help.

DO I NEED ANOTHER BOOKKEEPER?

Depending on the size of your business, you will have a bookkeeper, a team of accountants or something in between to manage your numbers. Similarly, in the online outsourcing world you can choose from the same spectrum of talent.

For the purposes of this book and the new system that it will help you to build, we encourage you to hire an off-site bookkeeper. Here's why:

It's important to embrace the notion that you don't need your staff within eyesight to have them working effectively. This notion will open up something to you that will allow you to build a business without limits. It will enable scale. To grasp this notion you need to see good results from just one staff member that you never, ever have to meet. Once you've seen that it is possible you'll feel comfortable to expand using a whole team of them, if necessary.

Your bookkeeper deals with the most quantifiable resource in your business – the accounts. Quantifiable things are easier to share online. They don't rely on facial gestures, body language or even colours. They just rely on numbers. Your bookkeeper doesn't need to hand-deliver a profit and loss report nor do you need to hand-deliver a shoe box full of receipts to make sense of the data that they contain.

This 2-day program is going to help you to digitise all or, at least, most of your data. This includes all of your financial data. Once your data is in digital format you can send it anywhere. Your bookkeeper doesn't need to be anywhere near you to see it.

Finally, and importantly, this book is going to introduce some concepts to you that are going to revolutionise the way you manage your accounting records. Your current bookkeeper may not have 'caught up' with the concepts that we are going to introduce to you. As comfortable as you no doubt are with your current bookkeeper / accountant, comfort always has to give way for progress to occur.

Note: if you are working with an accountant, not a bookkeeper, we encourage you to maintain that relationship. However, you will instantly save yourself hundreds of dollars monthly if you get a bookkeeper to perform those tasks that involve simple data entry and record management.

For those of you who have the Workbook, congratulations. This will be a very valuable resource. The first section in your Workbook will guide you through the steps to setting up your virtual workforce. You are going to love the results.

GET THE WORKBOOK NOW

Go to: www.catchupbook.com

For those of you without the Workbook, these steps are summarised below:

HIRE A VIRTUAL ASSISTANT

1. Browse the services available at:

   - elance.com
   - guru.com; and
   - odesk.com

2. Choose the site you like most and set up an account with them. You may end up using more than one but, at this stage, just choose one for simplicity.

3. Write your job ad. This is something that requires some practice. The Workbook provides a sample of the job ads that we use and the essential elements that yours needs to contain. In summary, you need to consider the following before writing the ad:

   - Tasks to be performed and the necessary qualifications of the person you'll hire.
   - How you will communicate with them.
   - Times that you will be available for contact.

4. Once you've considered these points, go ahead and write your ad. Unlike a printed ad, you can change it as many times as necessary while you monitor the feedback your

receive and the quality of your candidates.

5. Quick Tips:

- Write a detailed ad. The more accurately you describe your requirements, the closer you will get to fulfilling them.
- Rely heavily on candidates' references more than their own descriptions.
- Don't choose the lowest bidder.
- Include something at the bottom of your ad that they must refer to in their response so you know they've read the entire ad.
- Hire people part-time while you become accustomed to the process. Once you're confident, move to full-time hires.

6. Receive your applications, review, interview and appoint your first VA on a part-time basis. Set out your first instructions, provide solid feedback and build from there.

7. Enjoy the liberty that comes from well-delivered delegation!

HIRE A BOOKKEEPER

1. Use the same site for this professional hire as the one you used for your VA. Professionals want to see that you're a serious employer who employs and pays. It's good to build this track record on one site.

2. Follow the steps above for this new position, with the following addition:

    - Each geography will have specific accounting requirements. Make sure you find someone who understands yours. However, don't expect that you will only find this person in your own country. For example - many people in India have educated themselves on the unique reporting requirements of the Australian GST system so that they can serve clients in that market.

3. After reviewing the job applications, interviewing the candidates and appointing someone to the role, you now have someone who is waiting for you to complete the rest of this book. You will set up a system that allows you to communicate with your bookkeeper through your online accounting system and you'll

transfer your business information to them in digital format.

If you're going through these steps without the Workbook, you will find a lot of helpful resources on Guru, oDesk and Elance. However you do it, make sure that you've got these professionals in place before you move on. It's essential for the steps that follow.

8

BEGIN BY OWNING YOUR DOMAIN

It is not the strongest of the species that survive, nor the most intelligent, but the one most responsive to change.

CHARLES DARWIN

In this section we lay your online foundation. We will start with your domain name (your web address), we will digitise all of your data and then we will move to your emails and we will completely transform your relationship with that big ol' thing. This is a fun section. We leave the theory alone for a while, we roll our sleeves up and produce some great, tangible outcomes. First up – domain names ...

WHAT IS A DOMAIN NAME?

That is a perfectly legitimate question. However, I'm going to give you a rather condensed answer. There are books and computer engineering degrees dedicated to an in-depth study of what a domain name represents and how it directs internet traffic. I'm not going to bore you with that today. In fact, I'm going to keep it really simple. Heck, we only have 2 days to do all this!

Here's a simple way to think about domain names – think of your domain name literally as your domain. Your domain on the internet. A domain name represents who and where you are online. It's the space where all of your online activities happen. Like most things, a domain has a name – the domain name or, as some people will refer to it, the URL.

Your URL is the address behind which sits all of your online activities. For example – yourbusiness.com

If you had a filing cabinet and in that filing cabinet was every file that related to every single thing you did online there would be a big label on the front of that cabinet with your domain name on it.

There are 3 other ways that you will typically see a domain name used:

1. http://www.yourbusiness.com/example
2. http://mail.yourbusiness.com
3. info@yourbusiness.com

In each case, the domain name is just managing the flow of traffic to various files within your domain or your online filing cabinet. These addresses point your internet traffic or your visitors to locations where they will find different pieces of data.

Notice in the second example that 'www' was replaced with 'mail'. This is what's known as a subdomain. In simple terms, consider that www represents your domain on the World Wide Web (hence www) and a subdomain, in this case 'mail', represents that part of your domain that deals with just 'mail'.

You will see this sometimes on secure sites (banks, shopping sites). They will have www.yourbusiness.com and then when you are taken to a page where you need to add secure information, you will notice it moves to a subdomain. For example: www2.yourbusiness.com or secure.businessname.com

We'll deal with this in more detail later when we set up your emails and your websites because we will place some of those things on a subdomain. Using our filing cabinet analogy again, a subdomain would be the equivalent of another drawer in the same cabinet.

If you'd like a more in-depth look at how domain names work to manage traffic on the internet, I would like to introduce you to our good friends over at wikipedia. They'll give you as much boring information as you can handle on the topic of domain names, IP addresses and subdomains.

THE COMMERCIAL VALUE OF DOMAIN NAMES

Picture a line. On one end of this line is a local convenience store. On the other end of that line is, say, amazon.com

The local convenience store in our story is unlike most convenience stores in that it has a domain name and a website.

Exactly what for, we can only guess, but credit to them for trying to Catch Up!

Amazon, on the other hand, has a website, a domain name and we all know exactly what they're doing with it – they're gradually conquering the retailing world.

Now, do you think that there would be a difference in the value of these two domain names? Hmmm ...

What makes the Amazon domain name so valuable? Well, a few things but mainly it's got to do with how much business it sees.

By talking about Amazon and the convenience store, I want to make the point about domain name value. I want you to understand that there is a strong commercial reason for going to the effort of investing in your domain and taking the whole thing seriously. Here's a simple formula that will help to determine the value of your domain name and the keep track of it over time:

$$\textbf{DNV = (OV/V)R}$$

DNV = Domain Name Value

Online Visitors / Total Number Of Visitors x Gross Revenue

This formula measures how many people come in contact with your business through your online domain as a proportion of all people that come in contact with your business and uses that fraction to apportion revenue accordingly.

So, consider Amazon. How many people are walking into an Amazon shop and making their purchases in person? Zero. So, their online sales are 100% of their total sales. Therefore their DNV is equal to their gross revenue.

For the guy in the convenience store, let's just assume that no one goes to his website. They go to his shop because they see the shop as they're driving past. Therefore, his DNV is zero by virtue of the fact that no visitors are derived from his online presence. Not that there's anything wrong with that. It's just the other end of the spectrum.

In the case of, say, an accountant it will be interesting to watch over time as his or her DNV increases. Through following the steps in this book you will be able to track exactly how your online activities are leading to sales and exactly what proportion of your sales are run through your online domain. Handy!

But first, let's just see where you are on the spectrum. Which group are you in?

GROUP 1

You have a domain name. You have control of your domain name settings and therefore you can make changes to its settings. All of your emails bear the name of your domain and, of course, your main website bears the same domain name too.

GROUP 2

You have a domain name but it is not used throughout your business. For example, it may be the same name on your website but there are people in your business who are not using the domain for their email. You have limited control over the domain name settings.

GROUP 3

You have a domain name but you don't use it and you don't have control over it. You still send out emails with names like Yahoo, Gmail, AOL or, God forbid, Hotmail. You are reliant on others for the control of such things and it's likely that this person or people are not within your organisation.

GROUP 4

You don't have a domain name and are not sure how to obtain one.

If you're not currently in Group 1, that's OK. We will have you there by the end of these two days.

The importance of this step can't be overstated. Having control of your domain is essential because we are about to place some of your important business activities within this domain. Not having control of your domain is like not being able to answer your own phone. Your domain name is your new contact point for people to meet with you online. You must control it. The Activity section below shows how ...

In your Workbook you will find a corresponding chapter that takes you through the simple steps to controlling your domain. Please go there now and complete those steps. It will take approximately 40 minutes.

GET THE WORKBOOK NOW

Go to: www.catchupbook.com

If you are not using our Workbook, that's OK. Just follow these steps:

1. If you don't have a domain name already, think about the domain name that would best represent your business. Is it a word? An abbreviation? List a number of options that you could choose but bear in mind the following:

   - the best domain names have no more than 9 characters. For example: instagram.com
   - it obviously needs to reflect your business name.
   - .com extensions are the best option.

2. Go to one of these websites to register a domain name. They will become your domain name 'host':

   - godaddy.com
   - crazydomains.com

3. If you have a domain name find out who 'hosts' your domain name (most likely where you bought it from) and get contact details for them. Then follow the next

steps.

4. Order a DNS Hosting program from your 'host'

5. Your DNS Hosting plan will include access to settings that will allow you to control your own internet traffic - where it goes and what it sees when it gets there.

You've just established control of your domain name. This is a big step and it gives you a great degree of control over how you communicate with your market. It's not common. Not many people make this step. This gives you a decided advantage out there. Well done!

9

GETTING DIGITAL

UNCLUTTER, ORGANISE AND EMBRACE THE NEW CURRENCY

Man is the lowest-cost, 150-pound, nonlinear, all-purpose computer system which can be mass-produced by unskilled labor.

NASA IN 1965

THE LITTLE LAW FIRM THAT PRINTED

I came across a very successful law firm as I was writing this book. The principal lawyer at the firm had been practising law for over two decades. He was a very good lawyer.

However, in those two decades it seemed as though not much had changed. Faxes were coming and going, the printer sat there whirring away and paper just kept on piling up around the shelves.

Not to suggest that it was messy – it wasn't. In fact, it was immaculate. There was a place for every single one of the hundreds of pieces of paper that the printer spat out each day. Every folder was labeled and each folder sat in alphanumeric order on rows of shelves that covered one whole wall of the office.

Each week the stationery people would wheel in a new trolley load of blank paper which would eventually grind its way through the printer and end up on the shelves.

As the paper got too much for the shelving space it was bundled into archive boxes, put into a car and was sent over to storage.

Once in a while a car would return from the storage place with an old dusty box containing one or a number of old files. A lawyer would dust off the cover, open the box and rifle through the contents looking for a special bit of paper that was needed for a case or a client or for some other reason. Once done, the special piece of paper would go back into the box in the right folder and the box would go back into the car and the car would take the box back to the storage place.

As I watched this circular circus unfold I was intrigued. Just what was on these special pieces of paper that were granted a special place on a shelf in expensive rented premises and then granted a semi-permanent life somewhere in expensive, rented storage? It must have been important!

No. I'm afraid not. The majority of it was emails. Printed emails! Or it may have been letters, or plans or some other document. But each of these documents had one thing common – they all originated from a computer. All of them!

But despite being from a computer, they didn't remain on a computer. They came into the physical world as paper-based documents. Printed, in all of their glory. Printed, filed, shelved and stored.

I couldn't hold my tongue forever. I don't think I actually yelled but I probably raised my voice. I said – "STOP!! Stop the printing, stop the filing and stop that car driving around stinking up the planet for absolutely no reason!"

"Guys, you don't need to do this! The documents already exist. You don't need to print them out. They're as good on screen as they are on paper. In fact, they're better! They can be uploaded, downloaded, emailed or edited and they can be shared"

Credit to them. These guys, despite their years of printing, faxing and filing, remained open-minded. They listened and we turned their operation on its head, all for the better.

We left their storage centre alone. We just had to accept that legacy. But we set about scanning all of the documents in their office. We set up folders for these new electronic files, we enabled those folders to be shared by the whole team so everyone had access to them and we tagged each file so that it was easily searchable.

Plus (and here's the punchline), they discovered that so much of what they had on paper was valuable intellectual property. This data was worth a fortune. A lot of their work could be released as 'white papers' on the legal topics they dealt with.

It could bolster the content on their website. It could be sent to clients as a 'gift', as an expression on their expertise. It was highly valuable stuff. But, it was only valuable once it was liberated from the paper that it originally sat on. It was only valuable when it could be shared and it could only be shared once it was digital.

This chapter is all about the process of getting digital. It's about adding value to your data first and it's about stopping all the waste, second. It's a great step in the right direction. Enjoy!

THROWING A SPANNER IN THE PRINTER

Picture a printed, bound, beautifully presented report. It took days to prepare this report and it shows some fantastic sales figures for the last quarter from the regional team. This is the sort of report that will inspire others in the organisation. This is information that deserves to be shared. You want everyone to see this sort of report.

However, while that report remains on paper, in physical form, it is only of value to people that are in the same place as where the report is. The only way to share that report with anyone else, and therefore get value from it, is to convert it to digital form. In digital form you could share it with just about every human on the planet.

The same can be said for all of your data – your reports, your printed out emails, your contacts, your client files, your notes, everything. As long as they exist in physical form only and not digital form then they are no good to anyone, apart from you and only you when you and the physical documents are in the same room.

This chapter and the activities that surround it are all about converting from physical to digital form. For many of you the transition will be easy. Indeed, it won't be much of a transition at all. However, for others, the transition may be a little weird and perhaps a little painful. For anyone who has been relying on their hand-written notes for the last 10 years, there's going to be a real shift in your processes.

But before we embark on the 'work' let's find some motivation for the work first. Why would we bother with this step?

Well, look around you. If you're not in your office then picture your office. How does it look? Is it a sea of organised tranquillity? Or is it a chaotic jungle of paper? Even if it is a tranquil reflection pond without a hair out of place, you've got to be hiding that paper somewhere and, wherever it is, keeping it there is costing you a lot, isn't it? I mean, heaven help us if a client ever calls and requests a copy of the Garden Heights file from 2012!

However you manage your non-digital files they are a frightful burden. And that's just the storage side of things. What about trying to distribute copies of paper-based data to more remote members of your team. Say, your accountant.

Unless you convert from paper to digital, the value of your files is limited to just 1 physical location on this planet. As soon as they become digital then they can cover the globe, if you'd like.

Further, the case for digital v. paper is rooted in security. Whilst there may be some concerns about exactly who has access to the Cloud and everything in it, the reality is – you can't set the cloud on fire. And, ironically, nothing in the Cloud will get wet.

If your intellectual property and critical data is only stored on paper in your office it is more vulnerable to theft and damage than if it were stored on a super-computer server on the other side of the planet, believe it or not.

Finally, we make the case for digital because it's how you will run your business when you have caught up to everyone else.

You will produce everything in digital format, you will rarely print anything, you will communicate with everyone digitally and all of your business records will be safely, securely stored without requiring a single inch of expensive office floor space. Oh, and just think about the pure bliss that searching will become. With everything stored digitally it will just be a matter of tapping a few keys, typing a word or two and seeing your search results before you on a screen. No more dusty archive boxes, no more trips to the storage shed and no more paper cuts!

The activities at the end of this chapter will show you exactly how to get control of your data, how to store it safely and how to keep it backed up.

With this work complete, you will have transformed your paper into something extremely valuable – you will have created a knowledge base, whether or not that was your intention.

WHY IS THIS IMPORTANT?

Just imagine you were one of your clients for a minute. Your customers come to you with a range of problems and they assume that you have the answers. Most of the time you do. If you don't, you almost certainly know where to find the answers.

The history of work that you have just digitized, or are about to, represents a significant portion of your complete knowledge on the subject of your profession. If you don't believe me then consider this – what would your competitor or best client pay to get access to all that information. If the answer is more than $1 then you'd have to say that you have an asset there, correct?

So, being the responsible entrepreneur that you are, you know that, as with any asset, it's got to be put to work. You don't allow staff or machines to sit idle, do you?

It may seem a little premature right now but bear with me – in subsequent chapters we are going to use this asset to assert your authority. With it we will build your brand and your personal reputation. All of that information that you are making digital will have the ability to be shared. As it is shared, those who see it, recognise its value and those who benefit from it will want to get closer to its source – you. Let me give you an example:

THE GUITAR TEACHER

Let's say you are a guitar teacher. You have a number of clients / students. You teach groups during the week and you're a private tutor on Saturdays.

Let's also assume that for your weekday groups you have a syllabus that helps you to guide your students from beginners to maestros. Before each term starts you photocopy a new set of syllabus notes ready for handing to your class. In addition to that are your own notes that you have been gathering over time as you have held dozens of these classes. They are a bit rough but you know what they mean. They include the songs that people will learn in order, they highlight which particular parts student get stuck on and you've even got your own song that you teach which you believe really helps students to 'get' the chords they need to know.

Well, all of this may seem a little second-nature to you and, as such, you've lost sight of its value. You just roll it out each semester and you're content because your students are happy and progressing well.

OK. But what if *this* happened (I'm just going to whet your appetite here. This is where we are heading):

You scanned every single syllabus sheet. You also scanned all of your hand-written notes. You scanned your tutorial class notes for the last 3 years and you scanned a copy of your teaching song plus you played this song in front of your computer and recorded that as a digital MP3 file with you narrating throughout the song so students could follow along with you as you played.

Then, let's say, you sent all of these files to your VA (remember them?) via email and you asked him/her to re-type the notes into sequential order and then insert them into a graphically appealing syllabus sheet. She then sent you a copy of this in PDF format which can be sent anywhere via email or just printed at the start of each term. Then you asked her to upload a version of your teaching song to your website so that students could download it as a lesson.

So, now, in a few simple steps you have created some incredibly powerful 'content'. You've made your business present more professionally, you've converted thoughts on paper to lessons that can be shared with others and you have secured this data against loss, fire, theft and amnesia! Plus, you've outsourced most of the work and been free to carry on teaching your students – where the income comes from!

Some readers will race ahead with new ideas at this point, won't you? Like, some of you are thinking – "If I owned that guitar school I would make those lessons available online and charge a fee!" or "I would sell this new content to my current students on top of their tuition". If you were thinking anything along those lines, congratulations! That's exactly what you can do with 'content' and that's why 'content' is so valuable! For all of you and the rest of the readers who are a couple of paces behind, I hope you now get a sense of the importance of this step. Your well ordered data, converted to digital format, is a prize buried amongst your possessions. It's your acre of diamonds. Complete this section with diligence and you'll be strongly rewarded.

YOUR PEOPLE ARE 'DATA' AND THEY'RE WORTH A FORTUNE!

With your data sorted you can now move on to the second phase of getting digital. This relates to all of your contacts. It's time to start speaking digitally with everyone.

Of all the new behaviours that the internet has encouraged, the one that gets the most amount of press is the evolution from personal communication to digital communication. That is, rather than picking up the phone, mailing a postcard or just dropping by, we now fire off an email, a text, a Facebook message, a Tweet or even a Poke!

The younger folk don't raise an eyebrow, they just carry on poking and texting. However, for those a little older who are still strong on the phone and still love a hand-written letter, the transition can be a little drawn out. But, hey, when you arrive in France, you'll find people speaking French, oui? You've now arrived in the digital age. Time to start speaking the language.

In the digital age, communication is everything. If you're not communicating you're not known and in business if you're not known you're out of business.

But herein lies the opportunity! The greatest feature of a digital business is the ease with which it can communicate. To pick up the phone and call 1,000 people to let them know about your latest products is going to be a real effort. However, to send a beautiful, personalised email that includes this information and an immediate call to action is something that will take you only minutes to do. Provided, of course, you have opened up the channels to communicating digitally. And that's what this step is all about.

Just as you have created leverage on your data by turning it into digital 'content', you will multiply the power of your contacts database by making that digital and gathering it into a format which allows you to speak freely to your people, to remember exactly what you said, when you said it and to know exactly what they thought of your comments.

This digital database will open up many avenues to connect with your customers, clients, staff and suppliers but, principally, it will allow you to run effective email marketing campaigns and track your relationship with everyone in your database.

Also, the activities below will help you to gather your data from all around you and place it in one location. To see your contacts, know how many you have, know exactly where their details are stored and know by how much they have grown recently are essential metrics for the digital business. We start that process here.

Your Workbook contains the step-by-step guide to all of these Activities. Below you'll see a summary of these steps, in case you're not using the Workbook.

CONTENT

1. If you had the people power or the time, you would scan every single document related to your business. Although that is unlikely so you need to prioritise

the documents that you scan, using the following categories as a guide (these are all described in detail in your Workbook):

- accounting files for at least 12 months
- all existing agreements, contracts
- notable client work for the last 3 years
- handwritten notes
- images

2. Name all of your files. The naming is reasonably important but not critical. Your online storage solution will search every word in each document, not just the title. However, there are some important standards to maintain: (a) Be brief (b) Be consistent (c) Dates go first, in this manner - YYYYMMDD

3. Set up a folder on your computer and store all documents in the subfolders that match the categories shown above. We will come back to those later.

PEOPLE

1. First, stop and think - where are all of your contacts? They will be in places like your phone, your computer,

your notebooks, your business card pile, your brain!

2. Gather them all together in the one place - a spreadsheet. This spreadsheet needs to contain, at a minimum, the following headings: First Name, Last Name, Email, Phone Number.

3. Save the spreadsheet and back it up.

You now have Content and People databases. These are very powerful things. We will come back to both of these assets later and exploit their value.

10

IN THE CLOUD

ACCESS YOUR ENTIRE BUSINESS FROM EVERYWHERE

There was a time when every household, town, farm or village had its own water well. Today, shared public utilities give us access to clean water by simply turning on the tap; cloud computing works in a similar fashion. Just like water from the tap in your kitchen, cloud computing services can be turned on or off quickly as needed. Like at the water company, there is a team of dedicated professionals making sure the service provided is safe, secure and available on a 24/7 basis. When the tap isn't on, not only are you saving water, but you aren't paying for resources you don't currently need.

VIVEK KUNDRA, FEDERAL CIO, UNITED STATES GOVERNMENT

The server ... of death

I worked for a business a while ago and when I first walked into their office the first thing I saw was this huge black server tower in the corner of the room. It was not only visual. It could be heard too. A gentle, but obvious, hum. I ignored it initially but made a mental note – that'll be gone shortly.

Once I had gotten to know the people there a little better I leaned in during a conversation with someone and said "what's that?"

As though I was stupid, she replied "it's our server".

"OK" I said. "What does it do?"

Now, she didn't really know but she made a solid, exasperated attempt at telling me. "You know, it ... it runs our emails and it's our storage and ... you know. It's for all the computers. It's a server!"

This particular server cost thousands (about $25,000, in fact). What a shame it was now completely worthless.

THE CLOUD

You've heard everyone talk about it. But it's such an intangible term that it could be easily mistaken for more tech-nonsense, a fad that will come and go without you having to even raise an eyebrow.

But that's not the case. The 'Cloud' is one of the greatest revolutions in computing, quite literally, along with the internet. See, the Cloud is the internet. The Cloud describes where the internet lives and the Cloud is also where you and your business are about to spend a lot of time. Let me explain a little more about the Cloud …

Just picture a desktop computer. See the big black box? See the little green flashing light on it? See the leads coming out the back?

OK. Take that and simply scale it up by a factor of 20. It's now 20 times the size. Now, put it in a big room with 2,000 other boxes all the same size, colour and shape. You are now picturing a data warehouse. If you can picture it on an even bigger scale, you are now looking at a server farm.

There are enormous warehouses or 'farms' like this all over the planet. They are home to massive computers (servers) that contain unfathomable amounts of data including all of the data from all of the 100's of billions of websites that you search amongst on any given day. Plus people's emails, photos, files, videos etc, etc, etc …

After all, everything online is a digital file and every digital file has a web address. Websites are just a collection of these digital files that are 'served' up to you when you type in their specific web address. Your browser is designed to interpret and display these files on your screen. Firstly though, these files need a home and their home is these huge servers on these incredibly large server farms.

What we are doing in all of this work is moving your business files to a dedicated space at one of these server farms. I can't tell you exactly where. In fact, it will most likely be spread over several farms in several different countries. But far from having your precious data in some nebulous, cloudy type of environment, you will indeed be on the ground and highly secure.

Your data will be under constant surveillance. It will be located in an air-conditioned environment and will be protected from theft by some of the most advanced encryption technology available in the world.

But once stored in the Cloud, your data – your emails, your files, your contacts, your accounts, everything! – will be accessible 24 hours, 7 days and from anywhere in the world. I don't expect you to share my enthusiasm for this miracle just yet. But you will!

Storing data in the Cloud is cool. However, there is something much, much cooler. Let me just explain this fundamental concept about 'Cloud Computing' ...

I'm going to ask you to step back in time for a minute. Think back to the last time you ever bought software. Can you remember? It may be difficult. Most likely, it was an event you have been trying block out of your mind. If the software in question was something like an operating system you may have since had some professional counselling to help you get over the trauma.

Now, think about something far more pleasant – do you use a web-based email service at all? Gmail? Hotmail? Yahoo?

Have you ever logged in to your email service and noticed that the site had changed a bit? Something had been added, updated or improved?

Well, the email service you are using is still software. It's software in the same way that Outlook, Word and Excel is software. The difference is that Outlook gets installed on your computer and you access it by opening the program on your computer.

Gmail, on the other hand, is accessed by first opening your browser. Your browser then takes you to the server upon which the Gmail software is located and you access the Gmail software through your browser.

When Gmail (Google) think up a way to make Gmail better they access their software on the server that it lives on and they tinker with it whilst leaving all of your emails (stored in separate files) intact. Next time you log in to check your emails you are pleasantly surprised at how nice the new version looks ... and then you just get on with the business of sending and receiving emails.

When Outlook (Microsoft) thinks up a way to make Outlook better (rarely!), they rebuild the software in their office and then they create version x of the software and then they spend millions on advertisements to tell all of the users that a new version is available. You go to the store, buy the CD that contains the new version, you drive back to the office, you take a deep breath and squint your eyes as you gingerly approach the task of updating Outlook on your computer and, through no fault of your own, you proceed to wipe all of your emails off your hard drive and you tear up 15 hours of your weekend on hold with Microsoft tech support. And that's if everything goes really well!

That was a story of server-side software solutions (Cloud computing) versus client-side computing (software installed on your PC)

From this simple, but common example, I hope you can see why we would want ALL of our software to be hosted server-side – in the Cloud. Not just your emails (Chapter 10) but your file management software (Chapter 14), your project management software (Chapter 11), your account management software (Chapter 16), your client relationship management software (Chapter 12), your marketing management software (Chapter 13)

We want to give you the euphoric experience of never installing software again, always being the beneficiary of the latest version of everything, never paying ridiculous costs for software and folks I am hereby giving you permission … no I'm not … I'm giving you instructions to sack your IT department and delete the tech support phone number from your speed dial. Welcome to the Cloud – it's a whole new way of computing and Catch Up is your VIP membership! Follow me …

FIRST STEP - EMAILS

Our first step into the Cloud is to talk about emails. Emails can be considered the 'pulse' of a business. A business owner can gage a lot from the steady stream of emails that he/she receives. When his/her access to emails is restricted so too is the access that he/she has to up-to-date information from the business.

Some of the latest advances in mobile computing have been all about getting emails to a 'man in the field'. PDA's, smartphones, notebooks, netbooks, tablets and wireless broadband serve to bring emails (and other data) to the user wherever the user may find themselves.

That is wonderful and, no doubt, many of our readers will be the thankful beneficiaries of such technology. However, none of that technology is going to mean anything to any of you if you don't first have your data in the Cloud. As opposed to being routed through a server stuck back in your office

If one were to prioritize data, in a sample of 1,000 businesspeople, I'd say that emails would rank as the highest priority data for at least 900 of the respondents, so let's start with them and let's get your emails into the Cloud so that you can access them anywhere. Your other data will soon follow.

Firstly, we need to create a system whereby we have control of our emails. Most businesses have been sold on the idea that emails are a complex tool that require servers, expensive software and tech support. I am here to tell you otherwise. Emails and email accounts are simple. They are customisable without assistance from pros. They are cheap (usually free) to set up and you don't need a single piece of software. Anyone who has ever told you otherwise has not been entirely honest with you.

In this step we are going to set up a solid, reliable, scalable email system for your whole organisation. As the administrator, you will be able to view anyone's emails, you will be able to set up new accounts, close old ones, manage email signatures, forward accounts, anything that you may wish to do is entirely possible for you and you can do it without any assistance from anyone else.

Plus, the system we are going to set up for you will include a full suite of Cloud-based software tools including the ability to create your own websites, your own spreadsheets, documents and much more. This system is completely transportable. That is, it will work with exactly the same settings in your office in Canada as it does in your office in South

Africa. Such is the beauty of Cloud-based software services.

The easiest way to understand this concept is to talk about something you are probably already used to – Gmail, Hotmail and Yahoo. Chances are that at some point you've had an account with one or all of these providers. If you've ever travelled or have had kids who've travelled then one of these email providers was surely the tool that kept you in the loop while you were far from home, or from the kids. What we are doing with your business email is just the same thing but we are using an enterprise solution. Or, we are just using the 'grown-up's version'.

If you were (or are) starting a business from scratch you may be tempted to call your local IT solutions provider and they will come in, all guns blazing and they will tell you that you need a server, an enterprise version of Microsoft Outlook, an account with them so that they can provide 24-hour support for when (not if) things go wrong and they will call you every 12 months and tell you that you need to upgrade to the latest version of the software. Oh, if you should ever add another employee to the team, you'll need to call them so that the new guys' credentials can be set up on the system. Oh, and if you want access to your emails when you're on the road that's going to involve more hardware, a virtual private network, secure server settings, oh, and another upgrade.

I really don't have a high opinion of the guys selling this stuff and if you've bought their junk in the past, I'm really sorry but it's completely worthless now. The only redeeming news is that having experienced the pain that such systems cause almost all of their users, you are going to revel in the joy of using something far better, cheaper and usable.

Our system relies on software created by one of the world's best software producing companies. A company that you've relied on for countless operations before – Google. Your new email system is going to be powered by Google Apps – email (and other things) for business.

With Google Apps you will have an unlimited number of email addresses (or just one) and each one of them will be administered and visible by you. You will also be able to grant others (eg. your Virtual Assistant) access to your own emails so that they can manage them for you.

Because you now control your domain (Chapter 8) you can control the way your emails appear. That is, no longer does anyone have a reason for sending out emails using the gmail, hotmail, verizon, bigpond or yahoo domain. All of your emails can be sent out on your domain. It's free, it's easy and it's all managed by you. And with Google Apps you will have a user-friendly dashboard that gives you complete control over all of the emails in your domain. (Sounds like an ad, doesn't it! But there are no commissions here. Just one passionate guy chattin' to you about emails)

OK, you've done some great work on your domain name. You've wrestled back control of that thing. You've digitized your intellectual property and created some great content that will become very valuable to you and others. And you've got your contacts in a format that will enable you to light a fire under those relationships and keep them warm forever.

Your next round of activities is going to continue moving you forward. At the end of the activities below you will have your own email solution, Cloud-based, under control and it will be saving you a fortune when compared to the traditional alternatives. Please follow along with the steps outlined below.

This is where things get slightly technical but your Workbook will guide you through the process and make it easy.

GET THE WORKBOOK NOW

Go to: www.catchupbook.com

If you're not using the Workbook, it's still entirely achievable, it will just require a little more research. Follow the steps below and call out if you need help:

support@catchupbook.com

FOLLOW ME ...

Google has created an almost fool-proof guide to setting up your new email service. You really just need to follow the steps that their website takes you through.

1. Go to: www.google.com/apps
2. You'll see a 'Start Here' button. Click that and proceed.

Please note: you will need your DNS Hosting settings that you created in Chapter 8 and remember - we are here to help if you get stuck!

SOME PARTING THOUGHTS ...

If we can make your business' data available anywhere you are then the rest of your team could have the same access, couldn't they? What would that enable? Would it mean that you would still drag all of your team to the office each day? Would you still have such a big office? If your business' data could be accessed from anywhere, would you be able to work with people from all around the world? With anyone, regardless of their physical location? What would that enable? You'll discover more about this in the next chapter ...

11

Collaboration

THROW EVERYONE AT THE PROBLEM

It is a medium of entertainment which permits millions of people to listen to the same joke at the same time, and yet remain lonesome.

T.S. ELIOT, ABOUT RADIO

HAS ANYONE SEEN THE … ?

Most readers will have a team, of varying sizes. Even if you're a sole proprietor, you still collaborate with others on projects, eg the customer. When a team works together on the same project, that collaboration requires some organisation. Relying on emails will just no longer do. Let's look at a much better way …

A good friend of mine (Sally) runs a small, busy design studio. They have lots of clients and they're always attracting lots more. Sally is an strong adopter of new technology and we would always talk about business over a meal. Sally and I oftened talked about her business and we came up with an idea that enabled her to almost double her agency's productivity, almost double the revenue and she only had to hire one more person and that person lived in another country and came on part-time.

So, what were they doing? They were emailing clients. Back and forth, back and forth. A client would order a new website. They would do a mock-up, convert it to PDF format and then email this design to the client. The client would call or email with changes. The designer would do a new version and send it back. This would go on and on until no one knew exactly which version they were up to or who had approved the latest design.

Plus, if someone got sick, the whole project ground to a halt until that person got back. Not great!

Enter – Basecamp. An online project management tool that is like an online bucket. Everything related to a particular project is thrown into the bucket and because the bucket is online, everyone with the right password can see inside the bucket and search around in it. They can even toss new things into the bucket so that when the next person comes along to look inside the bucket, all of their contributions are in there.

This small design firm now uses Basecamp for every project they work on. It has even made it possible for the firm to hire offshore designers to come in to cover staff when the workload gets too much.

This chapter will show you some examples of how Basecamp gets used in business. It will soon become your favourite new tool for managing every client, case, file or project you work on. Promise!

WEB APPS

Do you recall our last conversation – about Cloud Computing? About how we want all of our software to be based in the cloud, not on our PCs? Well, staying with that same theme, we are going to refer to the sort of software that lives in the Cloud as a 'web app' – a web-based application. We just finished installing your first very tidy web app – Google Apps. Now we are about to implement another one and this one is excellent!

But first, let me provide some context. What are we aiming to achieve here?

In every business there are customers. In many businesses, the work done for customers could be considered a project. That is the case any time work is anything more than a simple transaction or where there is input required from the customer before delivery. In each of these cases, there is more than one person involved in each project because there is always at least you and the client. There are often many more – multiple people on the customer side and multiple people on the delivery side.

Let's look a few examples:

- A LAWYER RUNNING MATTERS FOR THEIR CLIENT
- A BUILDER DOING A RENOVATION
- A PERSONAL TRAINER HELPING A CLIENT REACH THEIR WEIGHT GOALS
- A MORTGAGE BROKER SETTING UP LOANS FOR A CLIENT
- A REALTOR SELLING A HOUSE FOR A CLIENT
- AN ACCOUNTANT PROVIDING ADVICE TO A CLIENT
- A THERAPIST WHO WISHES TO SHARE A PATIENT'S RECORDS AND NOTES WITH THE PATIENT
- A FRENCH TEACHER WHO WANTS TO SHARE CLASS NOTES AND HOMEWORK WITH THE ENTIRE CLASS

And on and on and on …

These aren't transactions, they are projects. They require regular interaction and communication between the client and the provider.

The sort of communication required for these 'projects' requires more than what emails and faxes can provide. Those methods of information sharing are linear and don't accumulate knowledge in one spot. They just fire data and documents at people, often indiscriminately. Have you ever been Cc'd in on a 10-week project that you're not heavily involved in? Not terribly productive, right?

Professionals yet to Catch Up are probably relying on telephone calls, email, mail and faxes to keep their clients abreast of project details. This means that clients are probably not abreast of the project details because the time and the effort involved in keeping people up-to-date using these mediums is prohibitive and, therefore, they don't get used and therefore the clients stay in the dark.

One of the best ways to provide value to your client is by delivering two things: (1) transparency and (2) good communication. Emails won't easily allow you to do either.

In the story about Basecamp above, I use the analogy of an online 'bucket'. Imagine that your project is a bucket and all of the details of that project get thrown into that bucket. The contact details of everyone involved, every document that relates to the project, any invoices that have been levied for that project, the objectives of the project, the major milestones of the project, your notes, details of phone calls. Everything!

Imagine then that this bucket, or repository, was located online behind a secure password. Anyone with the password could access the contents of the bucket. They could search the contents using intelligent filters, file structures and labels that kept everything orderly. And they could contribute to the contents of the bucket by adding their own notes, files, updates, comments, etc.

Then, when anyone accessed the contents of this bucket, they would see the latest contributions from anyone on the team – the clients or the professionals.

You can probably already see how using this tool, allowing clients free access to this 'online bucket' would be a rich, open, transparent and effective communication of information from the professional to the client and vice versa.

Let me put this into context. I've chosen 3 examples that shows how Basecamp has revolutionised different businesses. As you read through these examples, your job is to think about how you could use the benefits that come from Basecamp in your own business.

The three business examples come from: (1) a law firm; (2) an accounting firm; and (3) a design agency.

THE LAW FIRM

Throughout the process of running a client's legal case, at what point do you think a client has access to all of the information related to their case? If the file notes are hand-written and filed in folders that are stored on the lawyers' shelves, how does a client ever get to see those?

Most lawyers never share any of this information with their clients until the case is closed and the file is handed to the client. At which point, the race is well and truly run. And not always won.

Lawyers would argue that to share this information with their clients would be irrelevant and would take a lot of time. They assume that the clients won't understand the information and that there are no efficient means for transferring this data to clients other than, perhaps, email.

Both of those assumptions are incorrect.

The 'Messages' section in Basecamp allows a lawyer to record file notes, email dialogue, phone call conversations and the 'Files' section allows a lawyer to upload every file from a case to a secure storage area. This means that not only can they locate it at any time but so can the client. The client has a secure login and can browse their whole case whenever they feel inclined. Imagine it!

Most lawyers expect that this will provoke an avalanche of useless client dialogue and questions. Quite the opposite is true. The clients don't ask silly questions because they already have all of the answers – they can see it right there!

If you want silly questions from a client in any business, keep them in the dark and send them invoices for something they don't understand.

Until now we didn't have the ability to store data on an online platform that everyone has access to, regardless of their location. Now we do. So how long can lawyers (or any other professionals) carry on as though we don't?

Another great feature that comes about by storing data in an online hub like this is that colleagues can all access it at once, so to speak. If you have an office in Los Angeles and one in New York and these two teams are working on the one project then, regardless of the time difference or the physical separation, both teams have access to the same data and can equally contribute to the progress of the case. This is called collaboration. Imagine trying to share hand-written notes coast to coast.

Dear reader, if you're a lawyer / attorney, I'm a very keen advocate of this system for your business. Your clients will not know what hit them. This will do wonders for your relationship with them!

But I'm not done with law firms. I've got lot's more for you still to come! But let's talk about the accountant for a minute …

ACCOUNTING FIRM

Until I worked with an accountant who had Caught Up, I was a pretty bad client.

I would call my accountant from time to time and I'd ask some pretty dumb questions. I might ask – what was the total gross profit for January. He would take a few hours to respond to the email but eventually he'd come back with a number.

I knew that he was keeping a tally of how many minutes and hours he was spending on this mindless work because I would eventually get an invoice that referred to 'Miscellaneous time and attendance'.

What he was doing for me was going to my files, pulling up a profit and loss, reading off a figure and then either typing it on an email or having his assistant do it for him.

Either way, it wasn't advice. He wasn't adding value. He was just fetching numbers.

Here's how my accountant works with me (and his other clients) now:

Once my reports are prepared they are uploaded on to my 'project' on his Basecamp site. I get alerted via email that there is something for me to see. I log in and I see the prepared reports. Now I have immediate and constant access to this information. I can download it, I can email it to others, I can ignore it, heck I could even print it!

So next time I want to know the profit for January, I sure ain't calling up. I'm just logging in, which I can do from my phone, computer, internet cafe ... anywhere!

Plus, if I have any thoughts about the reports, I can simply make a comment which will go directly to my accountant but also be permanently stored on my file in the one, logical place – right with my accounts. Not in an email that will never be seen again.

Having access to my accounts like this isn't just helpful for accessing data but it's helpful for two other key reasons: (1) I am aware. I know what is happening, what has been done on my file and where my reports are. There is transparency; and (2) I'm saving money by not having the accountant chasing up information that is readily accessible by me.

Would I work with anyone the old way again? No way! Be careful accountants, your clients won't either.

THE DESIGNER

At the heart of things, every professional wants the same thing – to be well regarded for their skill, to be paid well and to be busy. If only there was a way to facilitate that while maintaining great relationships with your clients. Basecamp can help with that.

For the average person out there, going to see a design firm can be a hairy proposition. Dealing with such a nebulous craft is difficult, especially if it's not something that you do very often.

From the designer's point of view, dealing with clients for whom preparing the brief is difficult can mean that fulfilling the brief can be even more difficult.

From the initial brief to the final output, two things happen: (1) things change, including peoples' minds; and (2) different people contribute to the project along the way.

Both of those things are great but they can sometimes turn a project timeline into spaghetti.

Without a method that keeps the project on track, new ideas and new contributions can send the project into a million different directions. Then, when the final design arrives, if the brief is not met and the client is not happy, extracting money (let alone repeat business) from that client is a time-consuming diversion for the designer who would much prefer to just be designing.

I was first exposed to Basecamp when I hired a design agency in the Philippines. It was my first exposure to offshore outsourcing as well. So needless to say, I was a little bit unsure about how this was going to work. I was just expecting a barrage of email back and forth (and possibly a trip to the Philippines to sort things out if it got messy)

However, what transpired was a seamless flow of communication about my designs and my new website. I hardly spoke with the designers at all. I never emailed them. I would just log in to Basecamp and check the designs on screen. I would leave comments for them, they would reply and I could easily go backwards and look at previous versions of things and I could see the whole history of the project and everyone's contribution to it without bothering any of them with a silly email request saying "what colour are you using for the outline??"

When their bills came, because I had been a keen observer for the life of the whole project, I never objected to the amount. I would not have had a leg to stand on. Moreover, I just paid as a matter of course because I felt like I was an integral part of the whole thing.

So, let's say you're a designer, an architect. And, to date, you've been using some pretty archaic methods for communication and you decide to switch to Basecamp. Three important things will happen: (1) you'll empower your clients. When you arrive on-site, you're more likely to greet an informed, happy client with a clear understanding of your vision and the decisions that have had you arrive at that vision, (2) you're more likely to be paid on time; and (3) you'll more likely build your business on the back of referrals, word-of-mouth and positive commentary in social media channels (more on that later!)

A 30-SECOND SIDE NOTE

I know that there are programs out there specifically designed for lawyers, accountants and design agencies. For that matter, there are programs out there for just about every profession. However, if you're not using them now, there's probably a reason for that and it's either cost or accessibility. Most specifically designed programs will be cost prohibitive, especially for small businesses. If the cost is right then the implementation process may be exhausting, hence limiting people's access and willingness to become users.

Basecamp enters the scene and provides a simple, cost-effective, usable solution which will deliver at least 80% of the functionality that you require and you have the benefit of this book to show you how to integrate it with your entire online platform to make a seamless fit.

For most professionals, clients are largely a result of word-of-mouth referrals. Adopting a transparent, information sharing platform like Basecamp in your operations will have such an impact on clients' experiences that the word-of-mouth will be nothing but positive.

HOW BASECAMP HAPPENS

When you run through the simple set up process in Basecamp, you put in your basic business details. You load in your staff details, you create a profile for each of them – photos, email address, etc. Then, as you introduce your clients to Basecamp, you create a unique page for the 'Project' that you are working on with them and each person at the clients' company that you're working with gets a profile as well.

Whenever you make changes to the project, Basecamp logs the changes and then your clients are alerted by a short email which includes the basic details of the changes plus a link that leads to the Basecamp project where all of the details live.

If they want to communicate with you they simply reply to the email or they post directly onto Basecamp. Either way, all of your activity and all of their activity is recorded in one central place online. This gives everyone with permission the ability to access the details of the project whenever and wherever they choose to!

THE BENEFITS

I've emphasised the point about immediate payment several times. This, for any business, is so, so, so valuable. The pain of late payments is such that anything to avoid it is worth doing. The value of word-of-mouth is similarly valuable for business and, again, worth doing anything you can to achieve it.

You, the reader, can interpret many other benefits to the client experience that Basecamp will deliver and you don't have to think too hard to work out what they are. To access them all you need to do is become friends with Basecamp and then you just write your own cheque. You'll be as regarded, as well-paid and as busy and you like.

WHO ARE THESE GUYS?

Before you dive in, I'd like to tell you just a little bit about the group that have built Basecamp. Before you race out and start using their software, you may enjoy knowing more about who you're supporting.

Basecamp was built by a company called 37 Signals. 37 Signals have become the pin-up boys and girls for web-based software development in the last 8 years. They have an incredible following from users of their software and they have a readership of thousands (if not, millions) for their books where they espouse their business values.

They are proponents of many good concepts. One of my favourites is: less functionality means more productivity. One of the reasons that I like their software is because I can actually use it, and so can you. It contains every feature I am likely to use 80% of the time and none of those features that I might use 20% of the time.

They come from a stable of software producers that include others I will refer to in this book. All of them subscribe to similar principles and it's on that basis that I'm really comfortable in recommending their stuff to you. I have looked at just about everything and I have chosen what I believe is the best.

Just before I wrap this up I want to say one thing – I feel like a singing, dancing, writing cheerleader for Basecamp. Truth is, I am a fan but I'm only saying the things that I've said because I think Basecamp would be great for your business. I want you to know that I don't know the guys at Basecamp, I don't have any arrangement or relationship with them and if you choose to use them, I have nothing to gain financially, at all.

Now, on with the Activities. I hope you launch yourself at these with heaps of energy because the results are guaranteed to put your business way ahead of the curve.

Your Workbook has a section dedicated to your successful implementation of Basecamp. It's very simple to set up and use. The Workbook will also show you some tips on how to get the most out of Basecamp. One of the most important things is 'client adoption'. That is, making sure that the clients know you have it and that they know how to access it.

GET THE WORKBOOK NOW

Go to: www.catchupbook.com

If you're not using the Workbook, you can still do most of this yourself. As I said above, Basecamp is very easy to use and you will find your way through it quickly. Plus, Basecamp has a fantastic help section where users help each other solve problems that they come across. Plus, Basecamp allows you to set up an account for free to try it out. We say – just commit.

1. Go to: www.basecamp.com
2. Scroll down. You'll find that there's a lot of helpful information to get you started. Plus, you'll read success stories from those who have taken the leap ahead of you.
3. Sign Up. You'll have two months to try it out and get hooked.
4. Basecamp will intuitively take you through the following set up process.

At the end of this activity session should will have:

- set up your Basecamp account
- created your company profile
- branded your Basecamp with your logo and colours
- created your first project
- invited your first clients to access their project (very exciting!)

Just when you thought you had conquered the Cloud, along comes another great product from 37 Signals – Highrise. In the next section we are going to explore the concept of using a Cloud-computing solution to manage all of your precious contacts online. Come take a look ...

12

YOUR DATABASE I

ORGANISED AND AWESOME

Things should be made as simple as possible, but not any simpler.

ALBERT EINSTEIN

What's one of your most valuable assets? You might say – cars, equipment, property, cash, work-in-progress, etc. All of those things are very valuable. They spring to mind because you can see them and measure them in financial terms.

However, I'm going to say that your most valuable asset is your database – all of the contacts that your business comprises. Your suppliers, your staff, your contractors and, of course, your clients. If you lost every tangible asset in your business but kept your database you could always start again.

Surprisingly, the databases that most businesses are based upon are in poor condition, if they exist at all. They are often put together using Excel and are horribly out of date. In a lot of cases people refer to their Outlook contacts as their database. Few businesses have a centralised database that everyone contributes to. Most individuals in most organisations have their own private database and they take it with them when they leave! Plus, as the controller of a business, you may have no idea what state their database is in or what is being done with it.

So let's not do any of those things. In fact, here's what we want to do:

- have the details of every single contact in the one location, preferably online
- have all our contacts accessible by anyone in our business at any time
- track every activity involving each contact – emails, calls, everything
- set reminders for each contact to prompt the right actions at just the right time – an email, a follow up call, etc
- communicate with the whole database or certain parts of it whenever we want, easily

Not a problem! Your solution is called Highrise. Another quality software product from our friends at 37 Signals.

Highrise is a Cloud-based solution for client relationship management. It allows you to very quickly set up a 'page' for each contact and track everything that happens with that contact and because it's online rather than on someone's PC, everyone can access it and add details whenever they deal with one of your contacts.

In fact, whenever anyone from your team sends an email to one of the contacts you have placed in Highrise, that contact's page shows the contents of the email they received from the person in your team. Plus, when you and other people have a relationship with the one client, you can each see the latest events that have occurred with that client so you don't all end up calling them about the same issue.

LET'S TALK ABOUT SOME REAL-WORLD EXAMPLES

Here's a language school. It's called 'Speak Easy' and the business teaches a range of different languages to students. They have a range of classes starting at traveller-level beginners right through to advanced courses for professional translators and international diplomats.

The phones at Speak Easy ring all day with enquiries, which is great. However, no one has bothered to work out how many of the enquiries turn into paying students. Also, the business has been around for about 12 years and they have had many happy graduate students who have long since completed their courses but have not returned.

The Speak Easy database is ... well, there isn't one. In fact, when pressed, the owner of Speak Easy admits that the database really just comprises those phone numbers he has saved in his phone. The tutors keep the names of the students and once they've completed and paid for the course, their details are archived in boxes until they are allowed to be thrown away. Hmmm ...

In comes the Catch Up team with a head full of Highrise steam. Before you know it, Speak Easy has their act in gear. You won't believe the difference.

Now whenever an enquiry is made on the phone, the caller is taken through a very short script which helps Speak Easy work out what they are interested in. If it's a language that Speak Easy teaches then the caller is offered the chance to attend a free introductory session. To receive the details of the session, the caller provides Speak Easy with their cell phone number and their email address. Straight into the database, tagged 'Spanish Enquiry'

At the commencement of each semester, the names and details of each student studying Spanish are added to the database and tagged 'Current – Spanish'. During the semester each student on this list will receive emails promoting the

Spanish social events that the school is running. Once the semester is complete, each student's profile will be re-tagged 'Complete – Spanish' and until the day they die or re-enroll, they will get a monthly email advertising all of the advanced Spanish classes that the school is holding along with a graduate student discount of 20%

If you go to any one of the contacts' 'pages' on Highrise now you will see if they have ever been a student, when they were a student, every email they have ever received from Speak Easy, when they first enquired, any time they have ever called since, any time they have ever been called by anyone at Speak Easy, who they have dealt with at Speak Easy, basically every single time they have had contact with the business.

That's pretty powerful stuff, isn't it? Now, we're not going to win awards for any of that because that should be how every database is managed. But, it does sit in stark contrast to the way things were when Speak Easy has no database at all.

So now, what do you think is the most important part of the Speak Easy business? The chairs, the desks, the computers, the staff? No, it's their database, of course!

ONE MORE VERY QUICK EXAMPLE ...

A painter gets 100 calls per week. What do you think 70% of the calls are for? That's right – quotes. "How much to paint my bathroom?"

The painter could easily just say "oh we usually charge $70 per hour" or he could say ...

"Thanks for calling, we've actually got a complete list of prices that show what each room of the typical house costs. Plus it includes recent customer testimonials. We can send it to you straight away via email. Would that help?"

"It sure would, here's my email address"

Boom! Straight into the database

Now Mr Caller is getting an email from Mr Painter every month offering him tips on DIY painting, colour selections and every email includes a 15% discount on the next job that Mr Painter does for Mr Caller. Beautiful!

Mr Painter's database shows the date of Mr Caller's first call, the date of every follow-up email, the date at which Mr Caller finally decides to get the bathroom painted and every single call that goes between the two of them for the rest of their colourful lives!

Can I rest my case now and shall we just get on with setting up your database? OK great! Let's go ...

Your first step is to import your contacts. In Chapter 9 you digitised your contacts. You probably placed them all into an Excel spreadsheet. That's perfect. Highrise will allow you to import all of your contacts data into the program in one easy step. You'll be completely set up in no time!

Your Workbook covers the rest of the steps to getting started including the best way to tag your contacts so that you can communicate with groups of 'tagged' contacts separately.

Highrise gives you the ability to set up a free account to get started quickly without cost. For anyone not using the Workbook you will find the Highrise help section to be ... wait for it ... helpful! But, as always, we are here for you if you get stuck.

1. Go to: www.highrisehq.com and start a free trial plan.
2. Follow the prompts to import your contacts database from the spreadsheet you set up in Chapter 9.
3. Add some details to those contacts that you know and work with regularly. You'll instantly see the power of this program.

At the end of these Activities you will be so impressed with yourself and you'll instantly see how much value you have just created by doing this work. It's very rewarding.

But if you think your database is pretty hot, you ain't seen nothin'! The next section is where the real database magic happens. You actually get to communicate with them ... all at once! Come have a look ...

13

YOUR DATABASE II

SYSTEMATIC LOVE LETTERS TO YOUR CUSTOMERS

Words ought to be a little wild for they are the assaults of thought on the unthinking.

JOHN MAYNARD KEYNES

Everything that you're doing in your business is interesting. You may have done it so often that you've lost sight of that. But I tell you – it's true!

Your clients would love to know what you do. Some of them would love to know what you know. All of them need to know that you know what you're doing. If they ever doubt that, your value decreases (ie you get to charge less)

For you to truly 'Catch Up' or for you to truly embrace this new way of doing business, something is going to have to shift. You'll have to become transparent. You'll need to be open. You'll have to let the customers in. You need a relationship with them that provokes trust.

Plus, you have to discard any notion that your intellectual property, your know-how, your trade secrets are able to be kept as secrets. That includes your recipes, your 11 herbs and spices, your knack with a tool, your designs, your special sourcing arrangements. You have to share all of it.

Don't worry – I know there are some exceptions but far fewer than you may currently think. If you're hoarding your secrets as though they are providing you a competitive advantage, you're overlooking the fact that people probably have access to that information already, or they soon will. Also, it ignores the ever-present truth these days that things are changing so quickly that today's secret is tomorrow's history. You may as well leverage it now while it's still newsworthy. Let me show you what I mean …

Let's say you're a landscape architect. You build beautiful gardens but your clients almost certainly have a number of professionals to choose from when it's time for them to create a garden. So, how do you make sure that they choose you?

It's got a whole lot to do with trust. Early on in this book, we discussed the notion that people have two things in place right before they do business with you: (1) expectation; and (2) fear. The expectation that they'll get a great result. Fear that they won't.

If their expectations are greater than their fears, you're half a chance at winning the client. So, logically, we must do everything we can to give people the very clear impression that if they sign up with you, they are going to get a great result.

So, how do we do that? Well, you need give them a clear indication of what it's like to work with you, before they work with you.

"How do I do that?"

You build a relationship with them that allows communication between the two of you. That's the first step to trust and where there is trust, fears subside.

The by-product of the business that you conduct is the intellectual property that you accumulate. A tradesman builds know-how, a lawyer gathers knowledge about legislation, a hairdresser develops a keen sense of the latest trends and a landscape architect keeps on accumulating more solutions to people's outdoor problems. This information is extremely valuable. This is one of the most compelling reasons that people do business with you. It's because you are in the face of it all. You are immersed in your industry, your profession, the scene. Your clients can't be. That's why they hire you.

But how do they know that you are? How do they know that you're actually building any form of intellectual property or know-how? Well, you have to tell them. You have to show them what you're reading about, thinking about and learning. You have to tell them everything that you know.

HOW?

Simple – send them a regular email with all of the things that are going on in your business. It's hands-down the best way to establish your authority on your topic, to build trust and to eliminate your clients' fears that you may not be able to deliver what they need from you.

I know there are other mediums. I know about Facebook and Instagram and Twitter and other things and we're going to get to those but if there's a hierarchy, emails are primary and the rest are secondary.

If you don't have regular email communication with your clients, you are probably not engaged in the discipline of recording any of your intellectual property, your know-how. And if that's the case, you're almost definitely not sharing it with anyone. And if that's the case, two things are true: (1) you're not perceived as an authority, just a participant; and (2) it's only a matter of time before someone else steals the show in your sector, if they haven't already.

So, this leaves two reasons to send regular emails to your clients, about your business:

TRUST

As we discussed before, sales happen when expectations exceed fears. Or, when a relationship reaches a point of trust. Trust takes time to build. Trust is the outcome of regular communication.

The best way to get someone to trust you is for you to do something over and over, reliably. Sending an email to someone at the same time every week is a great way to signal to them that you are in business, you are reliable and you operate according to a schedule.

As you share your valuable information with them, as you expose your know-how and your genuine commercial concern for the recipient, you are investing in the relationship and building trust.

AUTHORITY

If people buy from people they trust then we want to be someone that people trust. Good relationships go a long way toward this but it's not about being great mates. We need to be regarded as an authority on our area of expertise. People trust authorities.

How do you become an authority? You talk about your topic. But it's not just about sharing your stuff, it's about having stuff in the first place. That's why we digitised some of your material in Chapter 9. You now need to continue that practice every time you create something new.

Here are a few activities that would build trust and authority in the case of a landscape architect:

Imagine creating a 10-video series on adding value to homes through simple garden improvements. 3 minutes each, simple tricks on a budget, uploaded to YouTube.

What about a PDF document that explains which plant varieties are best suited to the local area in which you work? Pictures, seasonal charts, watering and other care instructions. What brilliant material!

How about an article on a local sustainable furniture producer that you've used on a few jobs recently. Where they sourced their timber, photos of items in place, a message about the founders ... excellent reading!

What about a helicopter charter business?

Let's say you are a pilot. Let's also say that you run a charter helicopter business. Your customers want to know a few things about you but right up there at the top of the list of things that they want to know is – can I trust this guy to fly safely?

If you simply stick an ad in the Yellow Pages you will ultimately be forced to attract people based on price and they will try to seek comfort in the quality of the aircraft you fly to feel safe. However, if you have a website, a brochure, a blog and videos on YouTube that all talk about your impeccable safety record, the fun that your passengers all have and your commitment to your profession, your passengers will immediately acknowledge that you are an authority on flying. No longer will price be your competitive advantage but safety and fun will be. You can charge a lot for safety and fun!

The same applies to your profession as well. You must constantly be talking to everyone about what you do. The more you talk on your topic, the more authority you have.

Here's an example that's close to home – who is an authority on email marketing that you know? Wayne Butcher, right? Well I knew the same amount before you met me as I do now. You just know I'm an authority now because I'm talking about it.

What are you an authority on?

You have two dentists standing right next to each other in front of you. They went to the same school, got the same grades and have a clinic in the same neighbourhood. Which one of them is the authority on dentistry? The first one of them to talk.

You're the same. You might say – I'm a barista. I make coffee. There are a million baristas out there. What gives me the right to talk about coffee? I don't know any more than any other barista.

That may be true but remember this important point – your audience is not the other baristas that make coffee! Your audience is all the people that love coffee and want to know how it's made. You know infinitely more than any of them.

So, whatever your industry and profession, talk about it! Become the authority. You will most likely be the only one to do it in your industry, particularly if you are operating in a super-niche.

Videos, PDF documents, blogs, testimonials?!? Sound like a lot of work!

Let me assure you – it is MUCH easier than you think.

Allow me to introduce a good friend of mine ...

Her name is MailChimp. She's an email marketing program. Until I met MailChimp, I never would have believed that it was possible to fall in love with software. Well, as it turns out, it's entirely possible. I love MailChimp and I think you will soon feel the same.

MailChimp came to me after a long and exhaustive search amongst all the email marketing programs out there. See, I had arrived at the same point that you are at right now – I had my database, I was staring out at this digital audience and they seemed to be demanding that I speak to them.

I knew exactly what I wanted to say (shout about!) but I just didn't know how to make myself heard. MailChimp came along and I found my voice. Since then I have not only been singing and charming my crowd but I've been singing praise for MailChimp as well.

Why all this love for software? Well, it's not the last time you will hear me talk like this. There are other programs that I will introduce you to that have provoked a similar sort of emotion in me and it's about to stir in you too!

To date, you've probably become used to software war. Software war is when you install one piece of software and civil war breaks out on your computer while your software goes around murdering other programs to make room for its stupid self.

Folks, I'm glad to announce that PC peace has been declared. Harmony has been restored. Your software can now co-exist. In fact, your new software will talk to each other. They will be friends, they will work together for your common good.

I spoke earlier about the online gold-rush that is occurring. I spoke about the rush to serve online business with new products and innovation. A lot of this development is being done by a cluster of guys who all know each other. They might be from separate companies but they all go to the same conferences, they party together and a lot of them live within a few miles of each other. So they talk. They talk about their products, what they're developing and where they think the future is headed.

The outcome for us is that, if we pick software from the right producers, our software will be designed to work together and we will develop a synchronised system where data flows smoothly from one program to another. You're about to see this in practice ...

MailChimp loves Highrise. Highrise feels the same.

You've just finished preparing your Highrise database and it's looking pretty good. You're pretty chuffed. You ought to be. You wouldn't have thought that it could get even better but it's about to.

As you work through the activities below, you will set up your MailChimp account and you will be prompted to import contacts to MailChimp. Any guess where they are coming from? That's right – straight out of Highrise, straight into MailChimp! And if you followed the tagging steps in the last Workbook sessions then you would have created groups of contacts that will go into separate lists in MailChimp that you can communicate with separately, or all at once, or however you like.

MailChimp is designed to read your Highrise database and just drag across the relevant data. It all happens with a couple of clicks. All of a sudden you have a contact database and an email database that are both completely in sync. Any time you add someone to Highrise, with a click or two, it will update your MailChimp list. Brilliant!

Email marketing is so good for your business. It's basically free, it's easy (as you'll see below) and it drives business to your business. However, there is a major disclaimer that goes right here. We all know how annoying email can be and the last thing we want to be is a spammer! So, there are a few rules that we need to follow to avoid chopping 70% of our contacts out of our database the very first time we send an email!

These 3 rules will see you stay on the right side of your database and give you an audience that are very warm to your message:

1. When
2. What
3. How

WHEN

Often and according to a schedule.

There are many schools of thought on effective email timing but the best principle is to approach this in the same way as you would if you were emailing your friends. You would do it regularly, you would not usually do it after hours, you would know when they are likely to be attentive and you would have a pretty keen idea on what they wanted to hear about, what language is appropriate and the sort of content that will get their interest.

Here are some finer details on timing:

(1) Tuesday mornings at 8am is usually best (although MailChimp will help you optimise your timing based on your readership engagement data)

(2) Do it once a week

WHAT

Your audience will comprise people with varying interests. Some will prefer to read text, some will enjoy video and others will just want to scan through pictures. Although, guaranteed, everyone will enjoy a good story.

I believe your emails ought to be a mix of content to appeal to as many different interests as possible. Throughout the Activities below you will see the templates that MailChimp makes available for you. Using these templates, you can simply click and edit a template to construct a great looking email, just like you were editing a Word document.

MailChimp will allow you to choose from dozens of design templates and you will choose the one you like most based on aesthetics, branding and personal taste.

All of that is great but there are a few principles about content that we adhere to for effective email communications.

Our emails always include the following elements:

A light-hearted or dramatic cover story

An education piece (distributing valuable information has to be central to your communications strategy)

A link to your next webinar or event (more on this later)

A link to your latest YouTube video (again, more on this later)

A piece of news or an announcement

A link to your latest blog piece

In Chapter 22 we go into much more detail about how to produce all of this content. It sounds like a lot of work and, frankly, it will take some attention and time. But just like every good relationship – it will take an investment on your part to make it work. But the relationships with your clients are going to be the most financially rewarding of your life so they're well worth the effort.

HOW

Going from zero to email hero is a lot easier than you may think. In the Activities section below, you will open a MailChimp account, set up your list, create a template and be ready to fire off your first email.

With that work done, you are set. Every week you can simply open up your template, edit the content, change the links and click 'Send'. MailChimp will do the rest.

The next part of this process is the part that you will love the most. This is so much fun …

Have you ever sent an important email to someone? Maybe it was a business proposal, maybe it was a love letter. I can bet that for the next 30 – 60 minutes you could not concentrate on anything else. You want to know if they've opened it, you want a reply, you want some feedback. Anything! You've hit send/receive a million times. You may have even prank called their office just to see whether they are actually at their desk (!)

Well, if you're staring at a list of 1,000 email addresses from all of your extremely important clients and you fire off an email, especially your very first one, you are just going to be a ball of anxiety. But there is one unique difference with this sort of email sending.

MailChimp has an in-built feedback system that will immediately show you, real-time, exactly who opened your email, when they opened, how long they had it open for, what links they clicked on and whether they forwarded it on to anyone else.

You're going to want to set aside at least 30 minutes every week just to sit and watch as these figures come in. It is absolutely enthralling. You will feel like a spy. But more accurately, you will feel like a diligent marketer with a solid feedback system to gage interest in your content and each week you will adjust your content accordingly.

If you've ever wondered where the energy and motivation will come from to maintain a weekly email regime, this is exactly where you will find it.

Please enjoy these Activities below. I think you'll find them incredibly useful.

In your Workbooks, there is a section that shows you how to open your MailChimp account (for free!), how to set up your list and how to create your template. There are screenshots and links to helpful information all through this section.

GET THE WORKBOOK NOW

Go to: www.catchupbook.com

If you're not using the Workbook, you will still find it quite easy to navigate through the MailChimp website. Of course, you too can open a free account and use the software like anyone else can. We are here to help if you get stuck as well.

1. Go to: www.mailchimp.com
2. Go ahead and click on 'Sign Up Free' and get started.
3. Once you have done some exploring, click on the 'Lists' link.
4. Click on 'Create List'
5. Click on 'Add Subscribers' then ' Import Subscribers'
6. Choose the 'Highrise' option and follow the prompts to draw your Highrise list into your Mailchimp account.
7. Click on 'Templates' then 'Create Template'
8. Choose your template (we prefer a 1:3 column) and then begin to create your email template using the simple drag-and-drop editing tools.
9. Follow the prompts to send your new email to your list.
10. Monitor the response carefully to improve your next email.

We are making some progress folks! You have a digital database, you have an email list that is about to 'feel the love' and coming up next is a true computing revolution. Stay tuned ...

14

SHARING DOCUMENTS

FLAWLESS, FAILSAFE AND ... FUN?

Hardware: the parts of a computer that can be kicked.

JEFF PESIS

While I have been writing this book, I have spent 6 weeks in California, 2 weeks in Turkey, 1 week in New Zealand and the balance of the time in Sydney, where I live.

To write this book I have drawn on several different books, perhaps hundreds of articles and dozens of documents. Plus notes that have taken me months to prepare. I haven't taken my laptop or a hard-drive with me as I've travelled and, of course, traveling light doesn't allow for piles of paper. I am also working with an assistant in the Philippines who is doing a lot of the research for me. So how is it possible for me to access all this data without lugging it around? It's easy (and brilliant!)

I use a program called Dropbox. Dropbox is the essence of Cloud computing. It's a filing cabinet in the Cloud and it's going to be your liberation from piles of paper, earth-based filing cabinets, lost documents, location-dependence and "can someone email me the Kendall file?"

Dropbox will allow you to be anywhere and work from there, if you choose. Dropbox, and some of the other software that we discuss in this section, will immediately break the chain that means that you can only be productive or useful when you are at your desk. The same goes for anyone that works with you.

Dropbox is unique because it is based on your computer *and* in the Cloud. When you open a Dropbox account, you install Dropbox on your PC but you also set up a Cloud-based filing system.

The best way to think of Dropbox is to compare it to a bank.

Let's suppose that you had a bank account that you opened with Chase Bank at their branch in Solway St, Minnesota.

Imagine then that your money could only ever be withdrawn from the same branch. Any time you wanted to grab some cash, you would have to drive all the way to Solway St and make a withdrawal. PC-based filing operates in the same way.

Let's say you create a spreadsheet using your desktop computer. To make changes to that spreadsheet, typically you've needed to return to your desktop computer and access that file.

But we know that banking doesn't work that way. We can make a deposit into any Chase branch and then access our money at any other Chase branch, almost instantaneously. In fact, we don't just need to go to a branch to access that money. It's available using all sorts of different devices – a cash card, a cheque book, an ATM or even using online transfers.

Wouldn't it be silly if you could only ever access your money at the same place your stored it.

Well, some of you will be treating your data just like that.

Dropbox enables you to treat your data, your documents, your work, your materials the same as cash at the bank – available from wherever you happen to be.

Here's how it works:

When you open a Dropbox account, you install a small piece of software on your computer. You also set up a new folder on your computer called 'Dropbox'

Whenever you save a file to this folder on your computer, the Dropbox software recognises it and sends a copy of the file to your Dropbox account in the Cloud.

Whenever you change the contents of a file in your Dropbox folder, the Dropbox software recognises that change and updates your Dropbox account in the Cloud.

So that backs up your documents and that's important but there are a hundred different ways to do that.

Where things get very interesting is when you add different devices to the same Dropbox account.

Just as Dropbox is syncing back to your desktop computer whenever you make a change, Dropbox will also look for any other device that you own and will update that device with any changes that you've made to the content in your Dropbox folder.

LET'S SEE THIS IN PRACTICE ...

You happen to be building a spreadsheet as part of a presentation you are preparing with a colleague who works in the office with you.

You complete your part of the spreadsheet and then save it as you normally would but in this case you save it to your Dropbox folder that sits on your Desktop.

Then the Dropbox magic goes to work. Dropbox notices that you've made a change to your Dropbox folder and it automatically updates your Cloud-based folders that mirror everything you do in your desktop Dropbox folder.

Your colleague is working on another device which also has Dropbox installed and you are both members of the same Dropbox account – you are 'sharing' it. Therefore, your colleague has access to all of the files in your Dropbox folder as well.

Once you have saved your version of the spreadsheet, Dropbox syncs the online version and the spreadsheet is available to every device that is linked to your Dropbox account.

So, your colleague goes to the Dropbox folder and they open the spreadsheet you have built. Then add their part to it and save it again. Now both of you have access to the spreadsheet in its most current form.

Your presentation happens to be in Seattle so you jump on a plane with nothing but your iPad and a change of clothes. On your iPad you have Dropbox installed so that you can access all of your files on the go. When you installed the Dropbox app on your iPad, Dropbox noticed that there was another device requesting access to your Dropbox files so it pushed all of the files in your folder to this new device. And it continues to keep all of your devices up-to-date each time it syncs the files.

By the time you walk into the boardroom of XYZ Company in Seattle you have all of your files ready to go. You pull up the spreadsheet and take the audience through it. They are all very impressed and the meeting goes much longer than expected while you and the audience discuss the presentation. You edit the spreadsheet as the discussion unfolds.

Having spent a lot longer than expected, you are late back to the airport and barely make your return flight home. But in your hurry you misplace your iPad en route.

When you get to the office the next day you are terribly relieved as you turn on your desktop computer, you go to your Dropbox folder and find that the current, edited version of your beautiful spreadsheet is amongst all of your files in your Dropbox folder.

Do you see what is possible in this whole scenario? You have done 3 very powerful things. You have:

1. Collaborated (with your colleague in the office)
2. Backed up securely (despite having lost your much-loved iPad); and
3. Accessed your data remotely (during your presentation in Seattle)

This simple example doesn't do the whole Dropbox phenomenon justice but it does allow a peak at what's possible with this incredible software.

Let's consider the accountant ...

Many accountants work in small teams. There is often handover of a file from one person to another as it advances through the team. The bookkeeper enters the data then the file is ready for the accountant to prepare her advice and then the partners may want to certify that the advice is accurate before the file goes to the client.

Using Dropbox, these three members of the accounting team can access the same folder and look at the same files as each other. Any changes that are made are synced with each computer that is linked to the accounting team's shared Dropbox account.

Even if the office in which all 3 people work was struck by lightning late one night and burned to the ground, the files for the clients are all safe and sound. They are securely backed up online.

Some of you readers are already thinking ahead, aren't you? You know that when Nancy the accountant goes to her client's office she doesn't have to drag around her folders and files. You know that she can simply log in at her client's office and pull up the client's entire history, saved on Dropbox. You know that because you're starting to get a feel for the whole online thing, right? You know now that mobility is key, that location means nothing and that you could function perfectly from just about anywhere. What does that open up for you … ?

There are many, many Dropbox features that I haven't covered here but I hope you get a sense of the main ones. These features are the same that have allowed me and my assistant to write this book for you while we are on opposite sides of the planet and they are the same ones that will transform the way you work too. If you do nothing else with this book, please just go and open a free Dropbox account. The rest of your Cloud-based existence will surely follow.

The Activities at the end of this chapter are really important. They will help you take all of the data that you have digitised during Chapter 9 and upload it to your Dropbox folder so that they become accessible by everyone in your organisation. This is the point at which this data instantly gains value.

But before we go there, there is something else I would like to share with you. I'll be brief because I don't want to overload you.

However, this next tool is sitting right underneath you now so it's no stretch for you to reach down and simply turn it on.

You will recall from Chapter 10 that we have enabled your Google Apps email platform. I hope that this is already starting to pay dividends. Along with your documents that are now on their way to the Cloud using Dropbox, all of your emails are up there too so there will soon never be a time when you don't have access to your important business (or personal) data.

But Google Apps does not end there. As part of Google Apps you have been handed not just emails but Docs, Spreadsheets, Sites and Calendars as well. I'll take you through these quickly:

DOCS

Google has produced an online version of Word. They call it Google Docs. It allows you to create, edit and save your documents, completely online. Because this turns them into web properties or web-based files they have a web address just like everything else online. Therefore, sharing these files is as easy as sending the link to someone else via email. Plus, if you are collaborating with a colleague on a document you can both be working on it at once and see, real-time, the changes that each other are making. In fact, it's quite fun. You can literally watch their typing appear on the document as you are working on it!

SPREADSHEETS

Google has done the same thing to Excel. You can now build, edit and save spreadsheets online. You can quickly embed these spreadsheets into a website and have the public use the information contained in the spreadsheet too. Also, Google Spreadsheets has a thing called Forms. Forms are a spreadsheet with a questionnaire attached to the front of them. These questionnaires can be prepared by you. They can then be embedded in a website and the answers that respondents give automatically add data to the spreadsheet that sits in the background. This is the easiest way you will ever create an online survey.

SITES

Later in this book I am going to show you how to create excellent looking websites that help grow your business and cost very, very little to produce. However, websites don't need to be all singing and all dancing marketing magic. Sometimes you just need a website to announce an event, take a survey or to direct traffic to somewhere else on the web. For all those times there's Google Sites. This tool is part of the Google Apps suite of tools and it enables you to get a message onto the web in a matter of minutes. It's so easy your mind will run away with all that is possible when you can create and publish a website in minutes.

CALENDARS

I'll admit, one of the features in Outlook that is considerable is the calendar. It brings your emails and schedule together in one place. However, this basic feature in not enough to make an argument for Outlook when Google offers you the same thing … but better!

You'll notice that a theme running through this program is teamwork and collaboration. You'll see that everything is oriented toward working well with others. This is especially important when it comes to calendars. More than half of all entries in your calendar will involve someone else. Also, your schedule will often be given by what others around you are doing and their availability.

Google Calendars run on the same Google Apps platform that is powering your emails. It's 100% online and, therefore, accessible from anywhere and by anyone that is authorized.

This program is a full functioning calendar with every function that you're used to. Google is synonymous with the internet so you would think that the Google Calendar has got some pretty cool web-based features, right? Well, Google does not disappoint.

Your whole team can be given access to your calendar. This sort of goes without saying but if you feel inclined to share your calendar a little more broadly you can. Because your calendar is a web property it allows you to embed your calendar in a website and let others to interact with it on various levels. They can see when you're busy and they can actively make appointments with you online.

Digital data comes to life!

If you're still on the fence about any of this, I'd like to share something with could just tip you over.

You remember how you digitized all of your content in Chapter 9?

Well, the digitising process may have converted a lot of your paper-based documents to digital files and that's excellent. However, many of those documents contain text that, if extracted, could be used for all sorts of things.

It could be re-purposed for articles that you're writing for your email readership. It could be used to bolster your keyword relevance on your website. It could be used for future presentations to clients.

But to get the text out of PDF documents can be a slow process. Unless you've got a sophisticated scanning device and the know-how to use it, you might be forced to re-type all of that previously typed text. What a shame!

But, with Google Docs in place, all you need to do is to upload a PDF document to your Google Docs folder and Google Docs will run a reader over your document and pull out all of the legible text and provide you with a simple text-based document showing all of the words from your original. What a brilliant thing!

Convinced? Great.

Carry on then with the Activities below ...

Your Workbook will guide you through the steps involved in opening a Dropbox account. We help you decided which account to choose – Team, individual, etc – and we help you to quickly throw everything up into the Cloud in an orderly fashion so that it is easily retrieved.

One of the things you'll enjoy is setting up Dropbox on two devices and watching as your documents become available on both of them almost instantaneously.

The Workbook will also get you comfortable with the entire suite of applications in Google Apps including a walkthrough of the website creation process using Google Sites. This is a lot of fun!

GET THE WORKBOOK NOW

Go to: www.catchupbook.com

If you've made it this far without the Workbook, well done! This section will be a piece of cake for you. Opening a Dropbox account couldn't be easier and you're probably already comfortable with the Google Apps suite.

Go to: www.dropbox.com and just go ahead and click 'Sign Up'

In Chapter 9 you created a folder and some subfolders to house all of your digital content. We are now going to transfer that into your Dropbox folder and it's as simple as dragging and dropping them from your original folder to your new Dropbox folder on your PC.

DROPBOX

1. Create your Dropbox account and download the Dropbox software to your PC.
2. Locate your new Dropbox folder on your PC.
3. Now locate your digital content folder.
4. Drag your digital content to a new subfolder in your Dropbox folder.
5. Install the Dropbox software or app on another device

and 'Sign In' to your Dropbox account on that device.

6. Now open your Dropbox folder on your second device and view the syncronised content on that device.

GOOGLE APPS

1. Go to your emails in a web browser window (your new Google Apps-powered emails)

2. At the top right of that page you will see a grid of 9 square dots. This is a link to all of the new tools in your Google Apps software service.

3. Click on the grid and you'll see a pop-out window open up. Click on 'Drive'. You will now see a new window up and you'll see a button labelled 'Create'. Click that button then choose the 'Document' option. You're now creating your first web-based word-processing document.

4. Repeat step3 for each of the tools available and discover a whole new world of Cloud-based software that requires no installation, no upgrades and that also allows collaboration

> between you and everyone else in your organisation.

Take your time here, there are many cool features to explore and experiment with. If you need help with any of it, please shout. Otherwise, just go ahead and get the Workbook at www.catchupbook.com

The next section is one of my very favourites. As a student of Michael Gerber's, I'm a massive fan of systems. The next section shows how you can convert everything that your business does into a documented system. Have a look at how easy this is ...

15

YOUR OWN WIKI

EVERYONE'S KNOWLEDGE, SHARED

I have an almost religious zeal... not for technology per se, but for the Internet which is for me, the nervous system of mother Earth, which I see as a living creature, linking up.

DAN MILLMAN, AUTHOR, WAY OF THE PEACEFUL WARRIOR

SYSTEMS – YOUR ESCAPE PLAN!

Have you read the E-Myth by Michael Gerber? If you haven't, you need to. That book will change your orientation to everything that you do. Gerber coined the phrase – work on your business, not in it. He calls to account every entrepreneur who one day thought it would be a good idea to go into business but then got stuck working for a lunatic – themselves!

The E-Myth, amongst other things, espouses the critical importance of systems within a business. Systems will ultimately give the entrepreneur the freedom that he or she went into business to achieve. Systems allow the entrepreneur to teach the staff what to do and how to do it. Systems, processes and methods define the unique way that a business does what it does – how you mow the customers' lawns, how you write a proposal, where the paper clips are kept …

I read The E-Myth when I had my first business. I immediately took the next week off work and sat down and documented everything that my business did so that I could teach anyone how to do it and ultimately be free, while others ran the business, according to the systems that I had written.

The only problem with that genius plan was that no one could be bothered to read the pages and pages of system documents that I had written.

Now, however, systems don't need to be boring pages of text. Thanks to everyone's access to technology, they can come alive! They can be videos, audio files, images on a screen, animations and, of course, if you're working with a team of offshore tech experts, these things are very cost-effective to produce.

While that may be the case, where would one put all of these video bits and audio pieces?? Well, you make your own wiki …

WIKIS - NOT JUST FOR WIKIPEDIA

Have you ever heard of Wikipedia? Silly question, right? I mean, behind Google, Wikipedia is the go-to-guy for "Where is Mongolia, Daddy?" Wikipedia is the internet. It's a worldwide collaborative effort, it's constantly changing and being updated, it's FREE! it's accessible anywhere and it's rich with information – pretty much what the internet is all about.

But why should Wikipedia have all the fun?

Despite the depth and breadth of the information on Wikipedia, do you know that the wiki software it sits on is really quite simple? It's just a collection of basic web pages containing links to other web pages with a search function thrown on top. Simple. But isn't it always the simple things that are the most powerful? Heck, look at the Google webpage!

Wiki software is readily available to you right now. It is just a matter of setting up an account with a wiki software website and then writing up your own pages which become your own wiki online.

People do this for schools, scout clubs, sporting teams, community action groups and, of course, businesses. Anywhere that a collection of people need to access a common data source for information. What makes a wiki great is that it can be accessed and edited any time of day or night, anywhere in the world.

Wikipedia is the collection of the world's knowledge – a collaboration of what the world knows. Your wiki will be the same – a complete online collection of knowledge related to your business.

To get a sense of how your own wiki might look, you just need to picture Wikipedia but with all of the information relating to your business – your standards, your mission, your history, where you keep the coffee cups, where the staples live, your processes, your whole operating system. Indexed, searchable and editable, online.

In the Activities below, I'm going to encourage you to take every single thing that your business does and compile it all within your own wiki and give everyone in your business access to it so that the wealth of information that orbits around your business begins to gravitate toward your online wiki. Then your wiki will become the go-to-guy for every question and query that might arise in your daily business activities. For example:

"How do we answer the phone?" Go to the wiki and search under 'phone'

"Who is our paper supplier?" Go to the wiki and search 'suppliers'

"Who is our head of HR?" Go to the wiki

"Where do we keep the staples?" It's in the wiki!

"How much do we charge for this?" WIKI!!

"Where is the script we use for interviewing candidates?" Oh, for the love of God, would you just go to the wiki already !!!

Just in this short sample dialogue above you can see that the wiki actually became part of the culture? It became so that everyone eventually referred to the wiki and referred others to it as well. The wiki becomes the default. And that's exactly what you're after.

When the team knows that the wiki is the information source for your business, two things happen: you, the boss, become gradually more redundant. Secondly, the team begin to perpetuate the accumulation of intelligence that resides in the wiki as they contribute to it more and more. That is an excellent outcome. It means constant and never-ending improvement.

Your wiki will be every bit as presentable and functional as Wikipedia. The major difference is that it will show your logo in the top left. Your wiki can feature video, images and text. It is incredibly easy to set up and, even though you still may not agree that software can be fun, I bet there will be people in your team that do. And I can guarantee that these people and most others will much prefer to read through an interactive, online wiki to find out about 'how we do things around here' than anyone will be likely to read slabs of text in a dusty old ring binder from off the top shelf.

I am tempted to write 57 riveting pages on the topic of systems and how businesses can use a wiki to make their systems sing, but I won't. I'll just discuss one example:

STAFF TRAINING

Sometimes I love staff training but after I've delivered a training session 5 times I feel like a robot and, frankly, I start cutting corners. I race through it, I skip parts and I know that it actually gets worse the more I deliver it.

However, now with our wiki, our new staff get less face time with me but instead they go through a consistent program that is full of information in text, videos and images that gives them all of the knowledge that has been diligently prepared for them over time. Training takes less of our time because the trainees are sitting in front of the computer for most of it and I know that every time someone comes on board they are learning exactly what they need to know and exactly what we want them to hear.

YOUR WIKI EMPOWERS YOUR TEAM

Finally, I want to address the point that I made before about the team contributions. There is nothing more empowering for a team member than when they get to make a difference.

Seriously. Everything that you do for your team ought to be directed at helping them to feel that, in some way, big or small, they have made a difference to the business. There are few better ways than getting staff to contribute their ideas to 'how things get done around here'.

You know the situation too well, don't you. You see someone doing something that is just not in the manual. For example: they're using the wrong footer on that document that is about to go to a client.

You've got one of two choices:

1. You can have an argument with them about why they should be "darn well following the rules!"; or
2. You could acknowledge what they are doing and give them back the choices – "I see what you're doing there, Trevor. It's a little different to what it says to do in our wiki. If you've got a better way to do things you should probably update the wiki so that everyone is doing it the same way. Otherwise Trev, I'm going to need you to just do it the way the wiki says to do it"

The great thing about the wiki in this situation is that there is no excuse for not referring to it. I mean, most system folders are so far out of reach of most staff that just pulling it down from off the shelf is probably a breach of one of the workplace safety rules! But your wiki, on the other hand, is right there on your computer! You can't not know about it!

Good businesses have good systems. Your new wiki is the easiest way to build systems that become an integral part of your operations.

THE BEST WAY TO ACT BIG

Now, don't think that wiki-based systems are a solution reserved for big teams. They are important for a one-man band too. You can't remember everything about your business and, as a part of the Catch Up program, you are about to bring some new people into your business. You, like everyone else, need a way to train them with consistency and get them to contribute to your business and how it operates.

One more thing – your wiki ain't free. Sorry. This one's going to cost about $5 per month. There are free ones but you know me now – I've done the research. I've chosen the best one for you. But, by all means, feel free to browse around.

The Activities below will take you through the simple set-up process. This is another part of the program that delivers instant benefits. You will feel an instant sense of growth and development by just having this wiki sitting there waiting to be built.

In your Workbook there are the top 7 things that almost every business does on a regular basis. This will get you started and with this momentum you'll have a big fat wiki full of content in no time. Your Workbook shows you exactly how to open an account and which one is best for your business. There are free ones available but we actually recommend a paid version. You'll see why.

GET THE WORKBOOK NOW

Go to: www.catchupbook.com

Of course, you can still take this step without the Workbook. Just follow these steps:

1. Go to: www.wikispaces.com

2. Click on 'Everyone Else'

3. Sign up for your own wiki and then click on the 'Help' link at the bottom of the page. This will guide you

through the steps required to get started.

The next section is a topic that I used to really dislike – the accounts. But you'll see how I quickly developed a (borderline) romantic relationship with the invoicing. And so will you ...

16

ACCOUNTING

LIKE YOU HAVE NEVER LOVED IT BEFORE

I know what I don't know. To this day, I don't know technology, and I don't know finance or accounting.

BERNIE EBBERS, FORMER CEO, WORLD COM

A company I worked with a little while ago asked me for some help with their online stuff. As part of the overall process, I got to understand what they were doing with their invoicing. It was scary.

They had someone in the office who would go around to all of the professionals and sit down with them at the end of each month and transcribe their billable hours and match them to work done for clients. That person would then go back to their desk and prepare the invoices for the month. It would take them about 7 hours. Once complete, they would send a copy of the invoices to each of the professionals in the office to have them make sure they were correct. Inevitably the invoices would come back with many corrections. They would be re-typed and sent back to the professionals for final inspection. Hopefully this time they would return without red pen all over them and they could be sent out in the mail to the clients.

Of course, with paper-based invoices, once they leave the office they may as well have been thrown straight in the toilet for the amount that get paid without further ado. Paper-based invoices are an invitation to quibble – I never got it, I don't agree with it, you're charging me how much?!

Invoicing can be such a drag. This same firm literally had $300,000+ in unpaid invoices. Now this is work that had been done well and done some time ago. They deserved to be paid.

The same person who created the invoices spent the balance of the month chasing them and, in the process, she would undo most of the goodwill that had been developed with the clients. This is not a unique tale, is it? It happens everywhere! But it doesn't need to.

Sending out invoices by post just throws you into a queue with all of the other invoices that are unwelcome to their recipients. So why do it? Why subject your cash-flow to the standard 90-day risk? In the same way that you aim to serve your clients by being unique and competitive, you can adopt strategies that will give you their best attention when it comes time to pay as well as well as ordering.

The best way I have ever seen to get you straight to the front of the payment queue is Freshbooks. An online invoicing program that will save you thousands of hours, dollars and will actually enhance your client relationships.

You will recall I mentioned that many of our preferred software producers are building products that work well together. This product is one more of those products. Freshbooks integrates seamlessly with Basecamp to allow you to produce invoices for each of the projects that you are working on in Basecamp. There are many, many great advantages to invoicing with Freshbooks. But first, a little background ...

By now you would already appreciate that Freshbooks is going to be a completely online solution, Cloud-based and accessible from anywhere. You should expect nothing less :) You should also know that Freshbooks is available for free to get started.

Freshbooks works by turning your invoices into web pages. That is, you record your time, your fees and other details in your invoices inside of Freshbooks and rather than printing out the invoice and sending them in the mail (and hoping for the best) you just click 'Send via Email' and Freshbook does the rest. It has already imported your clients' details over from Basecamp so it knows exactly where to send the invoice.

When the client receives the email they click a link and they are taken to their dedicated page on the Freshbooks site that you have set up. It shows them not only their latest invoice but every other previous invoice and a current statement.

The lady who works in the office I referred to earlier used to get calls from clients all day. They would ask her to spend time re-printing invoices and statements and faxing or mailing them to the client. She knew that this was a ridiculous waste of time and she knew that 9 times out of 10 it was just a stalling tactic but she had no choice but to oblige.

When you start using Freshbooks these phone calls just stop dead. There is never any reason for any client to call to get a statement. They can access everything online.

Now, here's the killer feature – you know when you send those invoices out, especially the big ones, you basically just cross your fingers and count the time down until 1 of 2 things happens: (1) Payment (2) Dispute

Until either of those things happen you are basically left wishing. However, with Freshbooks you can log in to your account and you can see a list of all of your outstanding invoices. Next to each invoice is a label. It says 'Paid', 'Sent' or 'Viewed'

'Sent' means that you have sent it but it hasn't been opened. 'Viewed' means that it has been sent, viewed and remains unpaid. The whole concept of someone responding to a call for payment by saying "we never got it" is completely gone.

From the moment you send it, you know exactly what the status of the invoice is.

ONE MORE INCREDIBLE FEATURE

Most businesses will have a procedure for invoice collection because they assume that invoices won't be paid by simply sending them to the client. There will need to be a little bit of 'massaging' after the invoice goes out. This 'massaging' occurs in the form of more letters. In each case there is an effort made to print, envelope, stamp and post each letter. There is a cost to all of this.

With Freshbooks, this process is automated. Freshbooks knows when your invoices get paid and until they're paid, your client keeps on receiving automated follow up emails which you have pre-written and pre-dated. If you want them to go out every day after the first invoice goes out. That's fine. Every 7 days? Fine. Once a month? OK.

From Basecamp, where you work on the project, through to Freshbooks where you charge your fees, through to Xero where you run all of your accounting reports, your new system is based on a platform of integrated software.

Xero is an accounting system that is superb and, you guessed it – it's online, Cloud-based, cost-effective and accessible anywhere.

While you are preparing your invoices in Freshbooks, Xero is syncing with your Freshbooks account and drawing all of the invoice information across to your Profit & Loss Statements giving you real-time, up-to-date, online access to your all of your accounts. Xero even accesses your bank accounts (with permission) and draws out all of the data from your bank account and automatically enters it into the right accounts within Xero (after a little training from you). You've just eliminated a huge chunk of data entry time from your monthly tasks.

Again, one of the reasons we love online solutions is that they turn everything into a web property and, as a result, make them accessible and sharable.

But who would you want to share your accounts with??

Your accountant.

At the end of each quarter I DO NOT go visit my accountant. In fact, I don't even talk to him. He has the password for my Freshbooks account and he runs my Xero account. He prepares all of the required tax reports for me based on the current information in these two programs.

In the past I have had to email a copy of my accounting software file to my accountant, hope that he used the same software, wait for him to finish his work before I could do anything with my program again so that our copies remained the same. He would produce some reports in PDF format, email them back to me. He would make changes to the 'Master' file and then email that back to me. I would update my version of the accounts ... urrggh. It's hurting my head just thinking about it.

Now, at any point in time, I just log in to my account on Xero and I can produce a P&L in a matter of seconds. What a difference!

Now over to you – I'm really keen to see you experience the joy that your accounts can be with these two programs. However, I'm not an accountant, or a bookkeeper. Setting up Freshbooks is easy and it's something that you should do yourself. Xero, on the other hand, is a pretty powerful accounting program and, unless you're an accountant, I'm going to suggest that you get some help to make sure that it gets set up properly.

In your Workbook you will see the contact details for our recommended Xero and Freshbooks professionals. You don't have to work them, there is certainly no obligation, but we hope that you do.

In any case, if you just open a free account with Freshbooks and spend some time getting used to it, you are going to transform your relationship with your invoices and you will likely bring your debtor cycle back well within acceptable terms.

The Activities in this section are a great step forward in managing your accounts ...

Your Workbook will show you exactly how to open your free Freshbooks account and your free trial Xero account. You will also see some helpful links to professionals around the world who are advocates of these two programs and the sort of results they are able to produce.

We encourage you to work with one of these professionals to manage your transition to the new programs. They know our system back to front and they are the best equipped to help you stay on track with this program. Plus, adopting our love of outsourcing and efficiency, you will probably find that the professional you end up working with will be super-qualified, ultra-cost-effective and … not from your country.

If you are not using the Workbook, it's as simple as this:

FRESHBOOKS

1. Go to: www.freshbooks.com
2. Set up your account by following the prompts on their home screen.
3. Experiment with Invoice, Estimates, Expenses and Reports.
4. Customise your account with your own details, colour settings and logo.
5. Send your first invoice!

XERO

1. Sign up for your account at: www.xero.com

2. Watch all the tutorials and experiment with all of the forms.

3. If you're currently running all of your own accounts, you will have no trouble operating Xero. However, if you're currently getting support from a bookkeeper or accountant, it's time to get them involved now.

4. Make sure that you acknowledge the two programs have separate functions. Put simply - Freshbooks is for you to use, Xero is for your accountact to use. However, instead of your accountant having exclusive knowledge about your accounts, using Xero will mean that you have complete visibility and control over your accounts too.

This section is particularly important to get right. If you're not using the Workbook, please take some advice from your accountant or bookkeeper to make sure that this part of your Catch Up project goes smoothly. It's big.

17

YOUR WEB SITE I

$1,000, RANKED #1 AND YOU LOOK LIKE A STAR!

What, exactly, is the internet? Basically it is a global network exchanging digitized data in such a way that any computer, anywhere, that is equipped with a device called a 'modem', can make a noise like a duck choking on a kazoo

DAVE BARRY QUOTES, AMERICAN WRITER AND HUMORIST

THIS IS SOME OF MY BEST WORK

Let me be clear – I am not a web developer, I don't know how to code and I definitely don't know how to 'hack'. What I do know is that there has been a transition recently from websites that are just pretty pictures to websites that make money and I do know the difference between the two and I'm always glad to get the opportunity to help people make that transition.

What I also know is that building websites is a commodity-like service. That is, there are so many people around the world who can do it and do it really well that the price of getting one built is not what your local web design agency would have you believe. In fact, it's only a fraction of what they are trying to charge you.

This chapter explains how to make sure your website is a powerful marketing tool that helps to put a lot of money into your pocket and that building one of these powerful, great looking websites need not take a whole lot of money out of your pocket to start with. I hope you enjoy this chapter. It's one of my favourites.

ONE DIMENSIONAL WEB SUCCESS

A while ago, it used to be the case that you could just build a website and then tick the 'I'm online' box. These days, however – it's a very different story. Just having a website, no matter how fancy it is, is like calling 'Home Run' once you hit first base.

Your website is the hub of your online activity. It's where you want everyone to ultimately end up but to draw people to your website, you need to have a few oars in the water. That is, rather than just building a website, you need to build a web presence.

In this chapter, I am going to discuss the 6 key components that your web presence needs to include:

- YOUR WEBSITE – A WORDPRESS BLOG
- KEYWORDS & SEO
- GOOGLE PLACES, BUSINESS
- BUSINESS DIRECTORIES
- ARTICLE DIRECTORIES
- GOOGLE ANALYTICS

Don't worry. This is going to a brief overview. I don't think that your best efforts are spent becoming an online tech guru. Rather, I think the fundamentals are enough to get you interested, aware and active. After that, you're in the race. How fast you run is up to you.

Blogs are about sharing with authenticity. A good enterprise blog can help you really connect deeply with your customers in a meaningful way because the content is not only relevant but insightful and personal. I think most enterprises miss that point. When you do it right, your customerswill walk away not only having learned something new but will also feel much more connected to your brand.

DAVID ARMANO - POPULAR BLOGGER AT LOGIC+EMOTION

YOUR WEBSITE

A WORDPRESS BLOG

I once ordered a website. A long time ago. I chose my 4 favourite songs that I wanted to be playing on it when someone opened it. I demanded that everything on the home page be spinning around and flashing and I paid a lot of money to make it all happen.

3 people saw that website and out of all of them, my Mum liked it the most.

Thankfully, the process, cost and outcome of website development these days is entirely different.

You can still see some old relic websites that look like a disco on the home page. Everything fades in and out and then spins around and then reveals a girl in a bikini on the beach. The beach turns into a car, the car turns into a tree, the tree turns into letters that spell D-E-S-I-R-E which all fade into an image of the socks that you are trying to buy.

People spent fortunes on these sorts of sites and that has left a legacy for what people believe websites cost. How much do you expect to pay to have a website built? $5,000? $10,000? Would $20,000 be too much? No more than 12 months prior to the time of writing this I had a guy suggest to a client of mine that my client would be well served by a website that this guy would be happy to build for $60,000. It would sing, dance and it would enable my client to sell products online, run a blog and link to Twitter, Facebook and YouTube.

My client then sought my advice. I said the same website with the same functionality should cost no more than $2,000 to build. My client decided to save $58,000 and he ended up with a better site that he actually had control over.

I'm sure you have a similar story. It's probably even a little more personal. How much have you paid for websites in the past? Have you ever done a back-of-the-envelope estimate to show how much business you have derived from that site? Did it pay off?

It's not just cost that has changed on the landscape of website development recently. It's content. People don't want to visit an online brochure. They want to instigate a relationship with a business when they visit a website. They want to know about a business. They want to know its values, who else it is in business with, who its customers are and what it's currently doing. Sounds quite personal, doesn't it. It is nowadays.

A snappy remark to describe the change in websites recently is this:

> It's not a brochure. It's a conversation

People aren't visiting your site to see how much you can afford to spend on design. They are there to see what the quality of their new relationship with you is going to be like.

You'll recall that I spoke about trust a while ago. Well, when the prospective customer first visits your website, he or she is primarily concerned with whether or not they can trust you to (a) solve their problem; and (b) keep your promises. Spinning photos don't achieve either of those two things.

So, how do you build trust? As I said before, your visitors are looking to commence a conversation with you. They are going to listen first and then speak to you if they like what they have heard you say.

So, how do you get one of those conversations going? Well, you have to start it. You have to speak first and you have to speak as though everyone is listening and measuring whether or not they can trust you.

SANTA MONICA

I went walking on Santa Monica Boulevard the other night. It was my first time. I was amazed at the number of buskers that were there, all along the Boulevard. There were mimes, singers, dancers, magicians. Some were a lot more popular than the others but every busker had at least some people around them.

I watched as one busker arrived and was setting up her little area. She was an older lady who wanted to do some folk dancing, or something. I was interested to see how one of these buskers would get started from zero and build a crowd.

This older woman set up her little speaker, her little bowl for the money and she hit play on her little stereo and then she just started to dance. She was dancing for no one, just dancing.

She continued dancing for a while and I thought she was actually quite good. As people wandered by, most people glanced at her and kept walking but others (mainly older folk) actually slowed down and gave her a little bit of time. This stream of people moved past her at a steadily slower pace until some people stopped, bent over, flipped a quarter in the bowl and stayed for a minute to see the old folk-dancing queen. As the flow of people slowed and stopped, people gathered until there was a small ring of people around her. I thought to myself – so, that's how she builds a crowd. She just starts dancing.

I'm sure by now you've drawn a suitable analogy between Old Lady Dancelot and your website.

Most people will find it hard to just start talking without knowing that there is an audience. But to get an audience you've got to be doing something. Imagine ol' twinkle toes in Santa Monica waiting until a crowd gathered before she would start dancing! It would be a long night out there on the Boulevard.

"OK. So I've got to talk to the people. But how?"

We have the perfect tool for you – it's a WordPress blog!

I mentioned earlier that the price of websites has come down drastically. One of the reasons that has happened is because of the standardisation of the platforms on which websites are built. Or, in other words, websites aren't built totally from scratch anymore. They are built on what is called a CMS – Content Management System.

A CMS is like a kit home. It's the slab, walls and roof. Everything else is up to you – colour, design, etc.

You can choose different versions of your kit home – big, small, fancy, dull. You can even see it in practice by seeing what other people have done with the same kit and then you can say "yeah, I really like that but I want this and this too"

WordPress is the world's most prolific creator of 'kit homes' on the internet. A website built on WordPress has the advantage of giving you, the owner, the ability to control the content. Editing your website is as easy as editing a Word document. Getting back control of your site means you no longer need to pay your designer $3,787.50 to remove each spelling error.

There are other CMS's including Joomla, Drupal and still others but we prefer WordPress for its ease of use, it's popularity, the number of people that can work with it, the number of 'plug ins' available for it and the number of themes available for customisation. Some of these terms will make more sense when you read this section in your Workbook.

One of the things that WordPress is known for is being a blogging platform. This is another reason we favour

WordPress over others. It's because it is built for blogging and we believe that your website should be a blog.

We've already established that you need to talk to the people. The best way to talk to people online is to centralise your thoughts in a blog. Blogs are not personal diaries. They're not meandering thoughts from people with too much spare time. They are simply websites with pages that are built to change and be added to regularly.

The most common use of a commercial blog are magazines. Sites like mashable.com and even cnn.com are both built on the WordPress blogging platform.

These sites need the ability to change hourly, if not by the minute. Your website should have the same dynamic nature to it, albeit perhaps not so regularly but it should be different almost every time someone goes to it.

Sounds like a lot of work, hey? Well, it is a fair bit of work but building your business is always going to take some effort and developing your web presence is some of the most important business-building work you can do. I mean, what's the alternative? The Yellow Pages? I don't think so! Blogging is free, fashionable, fast and fun!

"OK, I guess I'm a blogger now then"

Yes you are. That's the spirit!

Bearing in mind that blogging is just speaking digitally and speaking to your people is all about building commercial relationships, what should you talk about in order to build the right sort of relationships? We think you need to talk about 3 things:

(1) RECENTLY WE...

Things you have done recently that made clients happy. This acts as a testimonial and testimonials are the most powerful form of self-generated word-of-mouth.

The most common examples of this are client success stories – Client A had this problem so we did this and then Client A had no problem.

(2) YOU MIGHT LIKE TO KNOW...

Things that will be of measurable value to your clients that you could usually charge for.

This is called the 'free advice' section. It's where you tell people everything you know and don't charge for it.

"What??!!"

Yep! A bit like this book. It didn't cost you much but it's a lot of valuable content for very little money. Of course, you are by no means obliged to do business with me but you know that I know what I'm talking about now. Before you read this book I could have won 417 awards and you still couldn't be sure if I really knew anything or had anything that could help you.

If you're a professional that provides advice, tell everyone exactly what you know and how you do what you do and don't charge them a cent. Instant trust. Instant credibility. Do it!

(3) HERE'S WHAT I THINK ABOUT…

Have an opinion and take a position on topics that relate to your industry.

That will probably involve picking some fights. For me, I have a healthy disregard for Windows, client-side software vendors, Quicken, Quickbooks and MYOB, traditional bookkeepers and a few others. It's good to polarize some people. It means you stand for something.

Here's a great saying:

I don't know a guaranteed recipe for success but I do know a guaranteed recipe for failure – try to please all the people all the time.

This part of your conversation should be reserved for upsetting anyone who disagrees with you. In so doing, you will bond with a tight group of people that feel the same as you. This creates fans way more than being nice ever will.

OK, we've made the case for blogging. Now to set up your blog / website …

Just using WordPress doesn't automatically make the price of a website lower. It helps, but there are still plenty of people out there setting up WordPress sites for their clients and charging them thousands. In fact, there are some companies who have built sites for their clients in WordPress and have not handed over the admin details for the site just so that they can still charge their clients an hourly rate to make changes – not nice!

Our approach is very different. We rely on the fact that there are literally thousands, maybe millions of people around the world who know how to build a WordPress site so we know it does not need to cost thousands. We also know that there are 'themes' that have been built to cover just about every single style, design and layout that you care to think about for your site. Building your site is really just a matter of deciding a theme, appointing a developer and then creating a list of customising changes that make the 'theme' into your very own new website.

How much do you think all of this would cost? Well, if you had it done in your home town, it could still cost $5,000+ However, if you use our team of extremely talented web designers, you can be up and running within 7 days and pay less than $2,000.

Of course, you don't have to use our guys at all. You now have access to an almost infinite pool of international talent from around the world at Elance, Guru and oDesk.

What is important though is making sure you prepare the right brief or instructions for your developer to follow. Most developers are capable of converting WordPress themes but the quality of your instructions will remove any potential problems in the final product.

To help, we have prepared an instruction template for you. You can find it in your Workbooks. Just download the template, fill in the blanks and send it to whomever you choose to work with.

Your Workbook also shows you the ideal layout for your website. Where to place the navigation bar, which pages to include, which features to include (and avoid). Once you have read this section you will know exactly how your website should look and you will be able to guide a developer to deliver exactly the right result for you.

Before we go on to the second essential element of your web presence, we have one last web-building story to throw your way ...

MAILCHIMP AND WORDPRESS UNITE!

No doubt you still remember meeting MailChimp. How could you forget?

Well, MailChimp knows WordPress and the two of them get along famously. In fact, one of the tools that MailChimp comes with, allows you to automatically build your database with details from the visitors to your website!

So, as you develop your web presence and you build your blog readership and you slowly build your legion of fans, every time someone goes to your website and wants to stay in touch with you, they simply enter their details into the form on your website and MailChimp grabs those details and adds them to your mailing list!

Then, every week, your new fans get the latest offering from your mighty digital pen!

In the Workbook, the website layout guide shows exactly where we think you should put this web form that attracts your visitors' details. Also, your design instructions template includes instructions to your designer that make sure your web form directs your web traffic to just the right email marketing list.

Capturing visitor data is the number one aim and number one measure of your web presence effectiveness. MailChimp and WordPress make it all happen for you perfectly!

KEYWORDS AND SEO

Hmmm ... how to cram the intricate science of SEO into a few paragraphs ...

OK, SEO – Search Engine Optimisation – is the science behind the way that Google determines which websites it should show to people when they type certain words into Google Search.

How they do it exactly is the study of many, many books and it is the practice of many, many consultants. However, I personally believe that people overcomplicate it drastically.

If you are targeting a huge market like "mortgages" then you have to know all about SEO and spend a lot of money being good at it.

However, we don't do that, do we? We are in super-niches. We are concentrating on small, profitable segments of the market that we can easily dominate. Effective SEO is one of the reasons we choose this path.

Your Google rankings are important. They will largely determine what amount of traffic you get online. So, we need to take this topic seriously. However, we can still take a simple, effective approach rather than getting too complicated about it all.

Think of SEO just like political interviews. Politicians just keep on repeating the same small collection of lines over and over because they know that they will be remembered for what they say most often.

If you follow the same approach, Google will recognise you for what you say most often and it will match you to people who are searching for the same thing. What you say and what your visitors are searching for are called Keywords. Keywords are those words that you must build your web dialogue upon. You need to constantly repeat your Keywords until you are sick to death of them, and then repeat them some more.

> *"You will grow bored of your own marketing long before your customers will"*

The process of effective SEO starts with Keyword research. No good carrying on about a Keyword that no one ever searches for. You have to know that what you're talking about matches what people are searching for. Keyword research is the name that describes the process of finding out what your target market are actually searching for when they are surfing the net. Keyword research can show, with incredible accuracy, the terms that people are searching for, how many other businesses are trying to own these Keywords and how their efforts toward effective SEO are going. All of this information will help you to work out which Keywords are the right ones for you to invest your efforts in.

Keyword research is a big topic but your Workbook helps keep it pretty simple with a few easy exercises that will help you immensely. You'll work through these at the end of this chapter.

Once you have found your Keywords, these words represent the frame upon which you will build your web dialogue. In the section above, you turned into a super-star blogger but before you go and burn up too much blogging rubber, you need to focus your content creation around those terms that your Keyword research shows up.

That means that rather than using a blog headline like:

"How To Fit Your New System"

You might say:

"Installing Your Gray Water Plumbing System In The Sydney Summer"

Your Keyword research may have shown up Gray Water Plumbing as one of your best words. You may also like to target your local Sydney market. A heading that incorporates your Keywords and your location will let Google know that this article will help anyone searching for Gray Water Plumbing solutions in your area.

You will not only title your blog posts this way but you will repeat your Keywords within the blog text, you will label your images with your Keywords, you will title your videos the same way and you will include your Keywords in every URL that you create.

KEYWORDS. KEYWORDS. KEYWORDS. KEYWORDS!!

Everything that you do will be centered around your Keywords. Again, the exercises in your Workbook will help you to successfully dominate the best Keywords for your super-niche. You can run through these activities at the end of this chapter.

Up next we are going to show you how to get one of those listings on Google that shows everywhere where you, how to contact you and what others think of you. It's Google Places (or Google Business). Come and learn about one of the best free online promotion tools out there ...

GOOGLE PLACES

You'll know of Google Places from your own experience but you may just not know what is behind it.

Google Places is the tool that helps businesses pop up in Google searches with location, contact and customer feedback information and you will often see these listings on the first page of Google.

Approximately 32% of Google searches are location-based. That is, the user includes geographic parameters within the search term. For example: "commercial lawyer in Seattle"

Based on this new and growing trend in search, Google created a product that would help users to locate pages containing information that related to their geographic search. This is – Google Places. Otherwise known as Google Business.

Despite the prominence that Google gives a 'Places' listing, few people make the most of this great tool to promote their business. Further, Google has made it incredibly easy to create your Google Places listing.

Your Workbook will take you through the steps necessary to create your Google Places listing and then some tips on how to make sure it is the first result that appears when your customers are searching for someone like you in their area.

As you may have gathered from the section on Keywords, your Google Places listing will be heavily punctuated with your Keywords but another important component has to be your content. Content, the quality, amount and consistency of it, is another important part of the algorithm that Google uses to determine who is going to appear on the front page of Google.

In your Workbook, you'll see how to create good content for your Google Places listing that will make your visitors know all about your business when they click on the page that Google creates for you.

In the next two sections, you'll see how content can be created everywhere, not just on your website ...

BUSINESS DIRECTORIES

Can you think of a business directory that might have once been used to help people locate businesses and view their contact information? If you go back, say, 20 years, there is really only one business that you would have been able to think of at the time – Yellow Pages.

Yellow Pages these days would have to be one of the toughest businesses to run at a profit. The amount of money it costs to produce and distribute those big, dumb books is so great that their advertising costs are always going to be far more expensive than online alternatives. For the cost of a small Yellow Pages ad, you could pay someone to create 100 listings in free (or cheap) online business directories and reach a far greater proportion of your market who are far more likely to be searching online than heaving one of those big books off the shelf.

Once upon a time, the Yellow Pages was a great medium but now that model has been copied and improved upon by online business directory services and there are many out there. Most, as I suggested before, are free. The rest are very cheap.

In the rush to create the most popular online directories hundreds of directories (or lists) have been created. The reason that so many companies have put an effort into creating business directories online is that they know the Yellow Pages model is dead and they are trying to replicate this old model online. But why would they do this and then provide the service for free? Because they sell banner ads on the rest of their site that is not taken up with the business listings. The more people that use their directory for searching, the more they can charge others to advertise on their site. Or, as some like to say – they are in the race for eyeballs.

This rush to build popular directories means you have the opportunity to advertise on every one of them in order to help people find you. Not only do these directory listings provide information to searching users, but they serve up information to Google's web spiders that crawl all over the web looking for content that is relevant to certain Keywords.

Google's spiders crawl these online directories as well and they will list these results alongside other pages that relate to you, your business and your Keywords. So, it would make sense to populate as many of these online directories as possible.

Do you remember what one of the first things we got you to do was? It was to hire a VA. Let me show you another great reason for doing this ...

Let's say that there are 50 online directories that you could advertise with. You can already begin to imagine that the process of listing with one directory is going to be very similar to the process of listing with another. This suggests that the whole process of creating 50 ads will be a bit monotonous and rather time consuming.

The choices are – do it yourself, have someone from your team do it or you could prepare some detailed written instructions and tell your VA to get it done.

Not only will your VA cost about 10% of anyone else on your team but you will get a much better result because you can afford to dedicate a lot more of his/her time to the task as it's only costing you $3 per hour!

In your Workbook you will see a list of online directories. Most directories will have a section for almost every business imaginable. You will see some tips on how to go about the task of creating your ads and making sure they look good. You can simply copy and paste these instructions for your VA to complete the work.

Setting up your online directory ads is an important part of building your web presence so take some time to do this.

You'll be well rewarded with increased traffic to your website and to your business.

This next section is also another easy way to develop content, get Google's attention, divert people to your website, increase your readership and build your database of email subscribers ...

ARTICLE DIRECTORIES

Again, picture the Google spider robot trawling the internet looking for good content to serve up to searching users. The more content that that little spider finds that relates to you and your Keywords, the more likely you are to appear on the first page of Google. So, the first order of business is to give that spider something to find.

On the internet there are huge libraries of articles on every conceivable topic known to man. For a person wanting to know about, say, African warriors, there will be someone out there who is writing about just that topic.

These days everyone is a writer. Because it is so easy to have material published online, everyone is putting digital pen to paper. Most people will do it for free because they are interested in exposure first and money second.

All of these writers need somewhere to publish their material. Some will publish it on their blogs to the attention of their readers, others will send it out to their list of readers directly but the name of this game is exposure so a lot of writers will send their material to online article directories – huge repositories for digital articles that include an advanced cataloguing and search system to help readers find the content they are after.

For your topic, no matter how niche and unique it is, there will be someone who wants to read about it somewhere in the world even if that someone is the Google spider.

The Google spider doesn't discriminate. It just reads and ranks. If you are writing about African warriors and your articles are visible online then when someone searches Google for African warriors you will be ranked according, amongst other things, to how much of your content the Google spider has been able to find on that particular topic.

So, how does this work in practice? I'm very glad you asked …

You'll recall in Chapter 9 that we asked you to digitize everything – contacts and content. If you have gone through that process, a pile of valuable content would have emerged from what was previously a lot of untapped intellectual property.

Some of it will need some work to knock it into the right format but almost everyone will have something they can post immediately as an article on these article directories.

There are certain tricks to this such as what to include in the heading, the first paragraph and the footer of the articles but once you know these, you can start laying out a well-lit path for your clients to follow all the way to your website.

Writing and posting articles online is a fantastic way to build traffic and authority. Despite how many people are now writing, there are far more who are not. Writers become the authorities on topics because they are the most outspoken and people pay attention to authorities.

So, seeing how easy it is (and cheap) to build your presence online, isn't it time to start doing so?

Your Workbook will show you examples of articles that appear in online article directories. It will point to the elements within them that make them effective so you can copy these parts for your own articles. Plus, your Workbook shows you a short list of the best article directories to post to.

All of this article wring and article posting seems like a heck of a lot of work, doesn't it. However, there are two important reasons why that is not the case – (1) you already have the content or are producing it as a part of what you do already; and (2) your VA does all of this for you.

Your Workbook will serve as a helpful guide for you to convert all of your digital content into valid search engine fodder or it will serve as a guide for your VA to do the same. Either way, you will understand the process and will be able to grow your web presence strongly because of this new knowledge.

GOOGLE ANALYTICS

OK. It's time to have some fun with all of this. Articles, Places, websites … it's all gotten a bit academic!

You wouldn't watch your favourite sport without being able to see the score, would you? If you didn't know who was winning it would reduce the whole exercise to just a lot of running around. Same with work. If we don't know what the result is or is going to be, there is little point to doing the work. For all of the work in this section there is a way to find out exactly who's winning!

The goal with all of our work in this section has been to:

BUILD A SPRAWLING ONLINE PRESENCE

DRAW PEOPLE TO YOUR WEBSITE
ENCOURAGE VISITORS TO SUBSCRIBE TO YOUR EMAIL MARKETING LIST
PRODUCE AND DISTRIBUTE VALUABLE CONTENT TO YOUR SUBSCRIBERS
DEVELOP A STRONG RELATIONSHIP WITH THE MEMBERS OF YOUR DATABASE

Throughout this chapter, we have been building your online presence. If that work has been effective, you will draw people to your website. To determine whether people are going to your website, Google has provided us with another amazing (and FREE!) tool to measure exactly how many people are visiting your site.

Not only this but we can tell how they got there, where they are in the world, what terms they searched to find you, what computer they are using (!), what they did on your site, how long they were on your site for, whether they purchased anything and a whole range of other statistics that put a yardstick to all of your online business building work.

This tool, Google Analytics, is amazing. Without it, everything you do online is guesswork. If you use it, you can precisely determine what is working and what is not and then adapt your approach accordingly.

Your Workbook will show you exactly how to set up your Google Analytics account and how to monitor your results. Do you know you can set up Google Analytics to track not just your site as a whole but each and every page on your site and see exactly how your visitors move about your site while they're there?

I introduced this section as 'fun' and it may not seem like a lot of fun just yet but watching your online numbers improve over time, getting an accurate read on your online success and watching as people pore across your material, is much more fun than watching your favorite sport!

It's time now to head into the Activities section where you will need to put these important tools into place. It will take some effort but all of it will be very well worth it. These Activities provide a summary on what we've just been through and how to make all of this happen for your business …

If you are using our Workbook, you'll enjoy the activities in this section. If you're not using the Workbook, use the steps below as a guide for the work that needs to be done:

1. Determine the requirements for your website. Make a list of items that successful websites typically include.
2. Get familiar with Wordpress and the concept of 'themes' then choose from a list of WordPress 'themes' that you can adapt to your requirements.
3. Find a developer to create your site.
4. Send them written instructions showing how you want your site to work based on a layout design that we help you to create.
5. Develop your list of Keywords.
6. Set up your Google Places (Business) listing.
7. Set up listings on as many business directories as you can find.
8. Upload as many articles as you can create to the small list of article directories that we will show you.
9. Install Google Analytics on each page of your website.
10. Type your primary Keyword into Google and see your business listed on the top of page 1!

If you're not using our Workbook, you can absolutely do all of the activities above. It will just involve a little more research and study on your behalf. And, if you decide to do it this way, you will develop a great repertoire of online business building skills.

With your web presence built, you now have a solid platform from which to speak / tout / spruik / promote / brag. To this voice you just need to add volume! Social media is where you'll find the volume knob. In the next chapter, we'll show you how to wake up the neighbours …

18

SOCIAL MEDIA

LIKE!

You can't buy attention anymore. Having a huge budget doesn't mean anything in Social Media...The old paradigm was pay to play. Now you get back what you authentically put in. You've got to be willing to play to play.

ALEX BOGUSKY, CO-CHAIRMAN OF CP&B

Don't worry; skills are cheap, passion is priceless. If you're passionate about your content and you know it and do it better than anyone else, even with few formal business skills you have the potential to create a million-dollar business.

GARY VAYNERCHUCK, AUTHOR OF "CRUSH IT", GARYVAYNERCHUK.COM

I think about half of my readers will be moved towards this book because of social media and the ear bashing they are getting about it in the general media. Social media is the hottest thing to happen on the internet since the internet and to be at odds with it or to not be using it due to a lack of knowledge would be making many of my readers nervous. The perception out there is that social media is here to stay and social media is an important part of the conversation in the market.

Both of those things are true. Social media is strong and growing and it's essential for all businesses to understand how to use it.

Social media is a beast. A huge marauding beast that, if used incorrectly, could potentially consume all of your time and energy and produce little more than a lot of small talk amongst personal friends and a few strangers.

This section is relief from all of that. It is a focus on the most effective social media applications and those that will provide the greatest return on the time required to use them.

Social media is, as its name suggests, a chat amongst friends. But just because we are using it for commercial purposes doesn't mean that we ought to be less friendly. In fact, the context for social media is strictly friendship. Your success with the medium will be determined by how friendly you are able to be with your audience. Just like your web conversations – the objective is to develop strong relationships of trust that precede and complement commercial transactions.

This section focusses on 4 social media applications that we think are the most effective and relevant to a business like yours.

1. YouTube
2. Facebook
3. Twitter
4. Webinars

YOUTUBE

For decades we have been trained to believe that people we see on screen are to be revered. Prior to YouTube, the only way you could get on screen was to be on television or in a movie. Now, anyone can be an on-screen celebrity. YouTube is your very own television station and you are the star of every show!

YouTube gives you the ability to create your own YouTube channel and upload all of your video content for others to watch. If you're not using YouTube to build your profile you are leaving a big visual piece out of your online business building activities. Let's see a real-world example of how YouTube can turn anyone into a star and turn a seed into a multi-million dollar tree.

Lauren Luke, a very ordinary girl from South Shields, Tyneside, UK, had a strong passion for make up. She would sit in front of her computer web cam and apply cosmetics to create various different 'looks'. She started recording these private make-up sessions and uploaded them to YouTube. Before long people started to watch.

There was nothing pretentious about Lauren. She was not pretty, definitely not intimidating and nothing about her video production was professional. All of this contributed to her success though and in no time she literally had thousands of viewers. Those viewers would watch Lauren on YouTube and copy the way she applied make-up. Lauren starting getting lots of positive feedback from viewers telling her how much they loved her and what she was doing.

Thousands of viewers have since turned into millions of viewers and now Lauren Luke has her own brand of cosmetics, a contract with one of the largest cosmetics manufacturers in the world and stores open in major cities around the world selling her line of make-up.

All of this is a result of her part-time project to talk to people about make-up on YouTube.

If Lauren can do this with no production experience, no 'fans' to speak of, no special equipment, no commercial objectives and no advice, imagine what you could produce!

Lauren Luke is only one of many people that have created a huge profile using nothing but online video. Gary Vaynerchuk, Keenan Cahill, Ray William Johnson, Will It Blend and others have all developed enormous personal and business profiles using online video. The chance is available now for you to do the same.

Not only does video create some appealing content but the content it creates is loved by Google. You see, Google owns YouTube and Google loves video content. No surprise then that when Google sees you have gone to the effort of producing video-based content, it gives you a much better ranking than your competitors who have limited their content to just images and text.

What we encourage you to do is continuously create videos for YouTube. In fact, we say that you should produce one per week. Not only is this building your SEO success but it is giving your database something to look at each week when they see your new emails, all of which will include a link to your latest videos on your YouTube channel.

The idea of making a new video each week sounds like an extraordinary workload until your realise that your YouTube videos will all be made according to the following rules:

- LESS THAN 3 MINUTES EACH
- NO PROFESSIONAL PRODUCTION IS REQUIRED
- NO SPECIAL EQUIPMENT IS REQUIRED (YOUR IPHONE IS MORE THAN ADEQUATE)
- NO MAKE-UP
- NO MODELS
- NO MESSING ABOUT

The value of these videos is their genuineness and authenticity. Just like people don't want to see a flashy website that is not a true reflection of your business' character, your YouTube videos must be the closest, rawest reflection of you that you can produce – warts n' all, as they say.

Videos, made into web properties using YouTube, are so easily transferable online that you can share your message anywhere in the world. YouTube will generate a link for you that can be emailed to anyone and a web code that will allow you to embed your new videos into your blog website as well.

Once you have the taste for video production on this simple, cost-effective scale, you will realise just how easy it is to share a powerful, dramatic, visual message with the world.

Your Workbook will show you how to create, upload and promote your new videos. This is some of the most valuable information you will get in this program. Video is not new but it is HOT right now and your audience want to see you using it. Get into it!

FACEBOOK

Mixed and maligned thoughts usually spring to mind when the topic of Facebook comes up. On the one hand it's full of young kids with way too much time on their hands. On the other hand, it's a tool that has united over 1 billion users on a single platform. It's put millions of long lost friends in touch with each other and it is the single most popular social media application ever invented.

All of that is lovely, but do we care about Facebook? Yes. We care about Facebook due to the number of Facebook users. Also because of the expectation that Facebook users have about businesses that they deal with.

You see, Facebook is all about friends and friendships and in Chapter 13 we discussed the importance of developing relationships with your clients and prospective clients. Used properly, Facebook serves up the potential for deep, familiar relationships with clients and prospects in a way that other forms of communication, including email, cannot.

Facebook is a big utility, capable of many things but to try biting and chewing the whole thing at once would be far too much to cope with. We are going to keep it simple, get your business started (if you're not already) and provide a bit of excitement around the use of it so that your Facebook activities become sustainable and ongoing.

So with that, let's take a look at just 2 dimensions to Facebook: Profiles vs Pages

PROFILES

For the sake of this section, I am going to assume that you have a Facebook profile. That is, you use Facebook, you have some Facebook friends and you are fairly familiar with how Facebook works. Not a pro, just a user.

My objective with this section of the book and the Workbook is just to get you doing one thing on Facebook – appearing on as many peoples' 'News Feeds' as possible. From there we can start doing opt-in pages, video uploads, blog links and all sorts of other fun things. But, for now, it's all about the 'News Feeds'

As a user, you will know that when you log in to Facebook the first thing that you do is to scroll down through a long list of little quotes and quips from all of your 'Friends'. You'll see everything from "It's a boy!" to "I stubbed my toe" in your News Feed. When your Facebook friends are an accurate reflection of who your real-life friends are then it's all pretty interesting. So you keep on coming back for more, and more ... and more.

My own experience of Facebook has gone through 3 phases. Phase 1 was reckless abandon. I mean I added every single person that I have ever come into contact with. I was a mad user. If I had a thought, everyone knew. The next phase was just abandonment. As in, I just completely ignored it. I was exhausted by it all and I got tired of it. My third and current phase is embrace. I now know that for me to maintain many of the friendships that I have with people, particularly those out of town, I just have to open up and let them know what I'm doing and I know I can't do that effectively with the phone or email. So, I'm back and I'm excited about it because, frankly, I love the feedback!

Embracing Facebook means that I'm more a part of people's daily consciousness than I would be if I ignored Facebook. People know what I'm up to and, if they care, they'll tell me and we'll have a dialogue about it and our friendship will be injected with a little more fuel for the journey. That's important, friendships thrive on regular contact.

All of this activity, mind you, is happening on my personal profile page. On *your* personal profile page there is something similar happening. You could now introduce a new element to your personal profile which is your business happenings. Your business activity could now permeate your personal profile postings and then all of your friends could know everything that is happening in your business. You could do that. It would be easy to.

But I strongly recommend you don't!

Anyone who is passionate about their business will inevitably make it a part of their personal dialogue. You will become known for what you are interested in. However, your friends are not your clients and you need to be clear about your message and who it is intended for. In short, you need another Facebook profile.

In the earliest days, Facebook was not as intricate as it is now. You either had a profile or you didn't. There weren't variations. Over time, however, Facebook and it's users have evolved. Facebook has noticed that a lot of people were trying to create business pages as personal pages so you would see things like – First Name: Coca, Last Name: Cola. Or – First Name: United, Last Name: Airlines

So Facebook created a facility for users to create a profile for entities other than humans – businesses, bands, clubs, community groups, etc.

Now you have a choice – you can still create a personal profile page using your business' name and details. It will function just like your own personal page but it will bear the name of your business. For you to develop a following, you will need to request that people / clients become your 'Friends'. Your 'Friends' will see your posts appear in their 'News Feed' and, if that's our only objective, this will suffice.

Alternatively, you can create a 'Page' specifically for your business that will function in a slightly different way. Read on …

PAGES

This is our preferred strategy. Your Facebook 'Page' will give you far more choices. I'll explain …

The main distinction between a Page and a Profile is that people don't become your Friend, they 'Like' you. And when someone 'Likes' you, every time you post something on your business page, that post will appear on their News Feed – beautiful!

So, in simple terms, rather than create a Profile and requesting Friends, you create a very similar thing called a Page and encourage people to 'Like' you. The result is still the same – we appear in their News Feed and we remain a part of their daily consciousness but the process of getting onto that Feed is very different.

I'm sure you've been to a website and seen a 'Like' button. You may have actually clicked on one or two of them. Doing so will instigate a few different things but the one that we will focus on here is that you become a part of that person's daily digest of information. This is a huge privilege and a powerful position.

Think about the company you're keeping – you are amongst the pregnant mothers and the stubbed toes! You're on the inside! You are their early morning news check and you're a part of their mental Facebook escape time when things get dull in the office. You're more trusted than a billboard and far more personal than a TV ad.

To the extent that you 'keep it real' and keep it relevant, you're now their friend and a regular part of their thinking. To the extent that you're solving a problem for them, you're absolutely their first port of call when things get commercial and a transaction is required.

This realm is sacred and it's one that many of your efforts need to lead toward. If the only advertising you ever did was designed to get people to Like you on Facebook, that would be a valid strategy.

The next two topics are going to be: 'How To Get Liked' and 'What To Say'

HOW TO GET LIKED

There are a few things that you can do and you'll learn these with us in time. However, here are the things that you will automatically do as a part of this program. They are the most obvious and essential.

(1) Like button on your Home Page

This sort of goes without saying. Thankfully, in the website template that you downloaded as part of Chapter 17, we have included space for a Facebook widget that allows people to Like you right on your website. This is a good start.

(2) Like buttons on your emails

We really have put some work into this program, largely in our selection of the right tools for your to use. MailChimp, your newest and best emailing friend, will plant a Like button right on every email so that your recipients can be Liking their way all over your newsletters.

WHAT TO SAY

So, you've got a vein going right to the heart and mind of your clients and prospects. That's great, but – what am I going to say???? It's simple – something and every day. The key is regularity and authenticity.

Facebook is never about plugs and promos. Your friends don't plug. Your friends share. All you have the right to do with this valuable attention is share. As soon as you convert peoples' News Feed to a billboard they'll move quickly to remove the advertising. That is, they'll 'Unlike' you.

Here is an example of the sort of material that an accountant might post on Facebook:

> *Latest tax legislation raises the tax-free threshold to $15,000. Very good for students!*
>
> *Client says "Thanks guys, you saved me $20,000 in tax". It's been a good day at the office*
>
> *Reminder to all: tax forms to be lodged on 25th August. Let us know if you need a hand. Free hour for all our friends on Facebook.*

If you're subscribed to this business' News Feed, you'd have to admit that they're probably going to be the first you'd call if you need some advice, right?

Some of the best advice that we deliver in the Workbook is all about how to get set up on Facebook. This section is invaluable. Whether you are coming from a standing start or you have made a start on this long ago, the information that you'll find in this section will make a positive difference to your business. Despite the millions and millions of existing users, getting your business onto Facebook will put you well ahead of all but the most progressive of your competitors. Embrace this, it will pay off.

TWITTER

Truth is, Twitter is pretty cool but like most social media, it can become an unproductive time vortex in the wrong hands.

We approach Twitter with the same single objective that we approach Facebook – get into the face of as many members of our target market as possible with relevant, authentic content.

We take a less aggressive approach to this than Facebook because we believe that Facebook content has a higher level of regard from its readers than Twitter content. But below is our 2-step strategy to Twitter:

(1) Follow button on every page of our websites

(2) Auto-tweet every email through Twitter.

Again, the value of our system isn't in the individual parts but in the value of the integrated whole. MailChimp shines one more time. Every email that you produce for your database will be automatically sent through your Twitter account as a tweet. Twitter and MailChimp automatically create a link to a web-hosted version of your email newsletter and your Twitter followers can pick it up online.

This is great for people who already have a Twitter account or indeed for those who are setting up from scratch. In either scenario you will be producing regular, interesting content for your audience.

In your Workbook you will see instructions on how to set up your Twitter account and how to link it to your MailChimp account. Both steps are uber easy but seeing your system lock together like this is also uber satisfying.

Finally, your Workbook includes some best-practice examples of how other businesses are using Twitter successfully.

WEBINARS

(We love these!)

Webinars have to be about the best thing that the web has enabled. If you've not heard of them or participated in one yet, you're in for a treat!

I bet one thing you have participated in is a live event or a seminar where you sat in a room with a hundred other people, you may or may not have been given a drink beforehand, the air conditioning may or may not have been just right, you drove to get there, you parked, you walked a little way. It may or may not have been raining. You really invested in the whole event with your time.

Plus, the people putting on the event REALLY invested in the event. They paid for the venue, paid for the sound guy, bought the cookies and the juice. And they played the anxious waiting game to see just how many people would turn up.

Putting on events is a big deal, not taken lightly by either the organisers or the attendees. Events are a great way to disseminate information. They are good face-time for commercial relationships, they show that everyone is taking the topic seriously and sometimes they're good fun.

However, for all of their value, they are bloody hard to make happen. There's now an easier way.

Using just your computer, you can broadcast a live presentation, including PowerPoint slides, to a live audience around the world!

Attendees log in using their own PCs and watch your presentation on their screen. As the presenter, you can even appear in person using the webcam on your computer, if you have one.

Webinars are the new seminars. No venue hire, no sound guy, no cookies and no juice! Webinars allow you to host an event of your choice at any time and as often as you can get people together. Plus, because it is so easy for others to attend, people are far more likely to attend and attend on a far more regular basis. If you had the content, you could host an event every day. If you chose to, you could run webinars for staff training. You could host a training event every day for your team and they could be based anywhere around the globe.

Just like a live seminar, attendees can ask questions and participate as though they were right in front of you. Unlike a seminar, however, you can mute the entire audience or individuals and you can record the event at no charge and send a video copy of it as a link to anyone in the world.

Do you agree with me when I say that every presentation you do from now on will be a webinar? And do you also agree that you're going to run one of these things at least once a month from now on? If not, it's just because you're not sure what you might say. Let me see if I can give you a couple of examples to get you thinking about how you might use webinars to make a strong connection with your crowd.

Let's say you are a chef and you operate a cooking school

teaching your students the best in French cuisine. You have a great little business, your students are keen but they're irregular. It's fairly straight forward to get them to come for the 'Basics' course but then your whole marketing effort is about getting them to the 'Intermediate' and 'Advanced' courses.

You're located in a lovely setting in the country, a 2-hour drive from the main city. The Basics course is not highly profitable but you do gather everyone's email address when they do this course.

Having had a wonderful time with you learning all about soufflé, your audience is warm and receptive to your ongoing communication. So, each week they receive an email with a variety of French recipes and stories about French cuisine.

Each month you invite each one of your email recipients to a free webinar where they will get to learn a new French recipe. There's you in the kitchen with your computer and webcam set up to point right at you and the food preparation bench. You're cooking and talking to them live on camera and there's them, watching, taking notes and dreaming of doing the same thing, thinking of when it will suit them to drive for 2 hours to come see you again.

You record each webinar and then package up 10 of the most popular webinar recordings as a free gift for anyone who signs up for the Intermediate or Advanced course plus you sell it on your website for $29 for anyone who can't make it to your courses in the country – 10 french recipes, with instructions. Prepared live in our kitchen. Watch, learn, cook!

Cute, hey?

OK. Now a little more buttoned-down – the physiotherapist.

Each month your friendly physio will spend 30 minutes with you, live on camera, teaching you all about how your back works. She will show you how to manipulate your own back, stretching exercises and what to do at work to avoid lower back pain.

The events are free and at the end of each event, each participant will be offered a free live consultation at the clinic.

OK. Even more buttoned-down – the lawyer.

Each month your friendly property lawyer will come to you live, online with information about how to maintain your property investments amidst a constantly changing legal background. In this 30 minutes you will hear about every relevant legislative change that has taken place recently and also a case study that shows how highly successful property investors are structuring their investment vehicles.

My advanced readers will have picked up on the fact that these events can be recorded and, as new students of online video production techniques, will have realised, these events are fantastic ways to create new, fresh video content. Each month not only have you hosted an incredibly valuable online presentation for your audience but you have also produced one more high-value piece of video content that counts towards your advancing SEO score. Not to mention the authority that this sort of gesture elicits within your market.

Let me give you one more example before I sign off for this section …

Let's say you're a carpenter. You specialise in renovations and home improvement. A lot of your clients are DIY home improvers. They use you for some things but try their hand at the rest, the easier things.

Your business is so heavily driven by costs because everyone is trying to save money. There is one way to stay ahead of the competition and preserve your margins – solve a problem other than the financial one. You need to prove that they can trust you to do a good, honest job.

So, each month you schedule 1 hour on a Wednesday night and you go into the spare room in your house. You turn all of the lights on, you set up your laptop right there in the room and you show people how to find a stud, screw into plasterboard, erect a dividing wall. etc.

What a way for your prospects to get to know you! And what a way for you to generate some credibility and rapport with your prospects.

In your Workbook we will get you completely set up and ready to rock with your webinars. You will open an account, adjust your settings and you will actually schedule your very first webinar. Now, the audience may be limited to me and your Mum, but that's probably the best way to get going. Start small, get massive.

This has been a big section. It's one that we are really proud of. We feel that we have taken social media and really picked the eyes out of it. Some people will have you buried in social media and all you will end up with is a lot of mundane conversation that will consume a lot of time. However, we believe that social media can really serve you and your business. We hope that you will make the most of the social media Activities below and embrace this new dimension to business. It can no longer be ignored.

Your Workbook sets out the steps to achieve the outcomes described above so go there now and start building your social media platform.

GET THE WORKBOOK NOW

Go to: www.catchupbook.com

If you're not using the Workbook, you can still achieve all of this. Just follow the steps below and spend a little more time in the 'Help' sections on each platform.

YOUTUBE

1. Because of your Google Apps Email service, you already have a YouTube account. You can log in from

your email window.

2. At the bottom of the YouTube page, click on the 'Help' link and search for the following terms: Share videos, Embedding, Uploading, Good videos. What you read under these search terms will equip you to create links to embed in your blog posts and your weekly emails.

3. Think about what content you would create for a series of 10 videos. What would you clients value the most? What would you like to produce the most?

4. Go ahead and make your first video.

5. Now upload it.

6. Embed the video into a blog post and drop the link into your next email.

7. You're a movie star!

FACEBOOK

1. Go to: www.facebook.com/about/pages to read about how you can go about building your own Page. Try to make your Facebook Page name the same as your domain name.

2. Visit the Pages of other businesses for inspiration -

Starbucks, Coca-Cola, Nike, Butterfinger.

3. Install your Facebook Widget on your website.

4. Link your Facebook Page to your Mailchimp account.

5. You will learn more about what to do with your Facebook Page in chapter 22.

TWITTER

1. Set up your Twitter account. Try to make your Twitter 'handle' the same as your domain name.

2. Link your Twitter account to your Mailchimp account.

3. Set up a link to your Twitter page on your website.

WEBINARS

1. Go to: www.gotomeeting.com

2. Click on 'Try It Free' then set up your account.

3. Build the outline for a 12-month series of webinars. What could you talk about each month? What does your audience want to hear about? What would you most enjoy talking about? Consider inviting others to present with you as guests.

4. Practice with the platform. Learn about how the recording function works. Learn about how to be

the 'Organiser'. Ask your audience for contributions through the chat window. Conduct a practice session before you go live.

Great work! The next chapter is your victory lap …

19

YOUR NEW MARKETING MACHINE AT FULL SPEED

Don't bunt. Aim out of the park. Aim for the company of immortals

DAVID OLGIVY "THE FATHER OF ADVERTISING"

CONGRATULATIONS!

You have now built a world-class technology platform upon which to base your future operations. You can communicate with a world-wide audience or with a tiny local niche. You can begin to forge strong relationships that will ensure long-term client relationships. You have adopted some of the most powerful software solutions with minimal ongoing expense. You have removed some of the other time and cash-consuming technology that was holding your business back. You have joined a new, mobile, aware and current group of business practitioners. You haven't just caught up with the rest of the world, you've overtaken most of them!

However, there is still a catch! Just like any high-performance machine, your new platform won't drive itself. It needs to do be driven. This next section is a high-performance driving lesson.

The next few chapters aim to keep your momentum up by providing some basic activities that will help you and your team use your new system. As we spoke about in the very first chapter, adopting new technology is sometimes a challenge, particularly when it hasn't been part of the culture in the past. You and your team need to see the benefits quickly in order for everyone to embrace the technology. The activities in this section are designed to help everyone see not only the benefits but to also see an assertive adoption of the technology by the team's leader – you.

In this chapter, we are going to focus on your social media channels and the content that goes into them.

If you have followed the Activities in the preceding chapters, you are now in charge of a full suite of social media tools that will allow you to blast a message out to the world.

As tempting as it is to simply yell at everyone with discount offers and statements about how good you are, that may deliver the exact opposite of what you're hoping to achieve. Social media has its own unique rules that will determine how successful you are going to be. Social media is competitive. There's a lot of other people out there competing for the attention of your market. Just like any other competition – it's important to play by the rules.

Social media is a powerful communications tool. But it can't be approached with traditional marketing messages and positioning. In the social media world, chest-thumping and "me, me, me" marketing is the fastest way to send your audience packing

REBEL BROWN, AUTHOR

All of your content will be produced and delivered according to these 3 rules:

1. Adding content can't be done on an ad hoc basis. It must be done according to a plan or it won't get done at all. To help you with this, the Activities below contain advice on how to create your 'Content Plan'. Your Content Plan will be your guide for how to run your new system. Think of it like an Operator's Manual.

2. Your content and its theme must be consistent. You will attract followers by what you do. If you change your theme, you will confuse and then lose your followers. Once a theme (and your Keywords) have been decided upon, it must remain constant.

3. Your content must be added on a regular basis. Whether this is content for your social media channels or just internal content being added to Freshbooks, it must happen according to a pre-determined schedule. This is the only way that all the system's users will be able to rely on it.

CONTENT PLAN

To manage all of the activities happening on your social media platform, you will need a plan. We'd love to help you build that plan so that you get the most out of your new system.

YOUR SOCIAL MEDIA ACTIVITIES WILL INCLUDE THE FOLLOWING:

- CREATING BLOG POSTS
- POSTING TO FACEBOOK AND TWITTER
- POSTING YOUTUBE VIDEOS
- CREATING WEBINARS
- DISTRIBUTING REGULAR EMAIL MATERIAL
- CHECKING YOUR DATABASE SUBSCRIBER NUMBERS; AND
- MAINTAINING YOUR SEO SCORES BY CONTINUALLY PUBLISHING DATA

Sounds a bit exhausting, doesn't it! Don't worry – once a part of your regular routine, it will be second nature and you will enjoy all of it. Plus, your new Content Plan will be your perfect partner throughout.

The Content Plan is broken up into three sections:

1. Guideline
2. Sources
3. Keywords

GUIDELINE

Social media can be a bit bewildering. If you're inclined to get distracted, social media will prove to be your greatest distraction. There is so much to see and do, you will wonder where to begin and you will never, ever find the end. So, it's best to start with a guideline that keeps your activities focussed on your target market.

Your Guideline will be a clear description of what you are trying to achieve, who you want to talk to and a description of the information you will deliver.

One of the most powerful things about your new digital platform is that just about everything can be measured – clicks, opens, forwards, exits, everything. This is true for your social media tools as well.

Rather than a random guess at who your market is or what you are trying to achieve, you will describe these things in detail so that you can then measure just how effective your social media network is. Your guideline will be expressed mainly in numbers and confined categories.

SOURCES

One of the things that stops people from being active in their social media network is that they run out of content. They get digitally tongue-tied. The result is that their audience loses interest, they stop getting any feedback and they declare the medium a waste of time.

The best way to avoid this is to know where your content is going to come from, well in advance. You will typically have two sources of information - original and interpreted.

Original information is information that you have prepared from your own data, experiences and knowledge. A lot of the digitised data that you prepared in Chapter 9 will provide your original content. Original content, I might add, is the most valuable content you will produce.

Interpreted content is your interpretation of information that others have produced. For example, you may read an article on a topic that you know your readers will enjoy. You will provide links to this article and your opinion on the information. You may also prepare an interpretative piece based on several articles that you have come across. Interpreted data will probably represent most of the content that you produce.

Your Content Plan will list the sources of your original and interpreted content so that you know where to go to find more inspiration when your Content Plan dictates that it is time for another piece.

KEYWORDS

Your Content Plan contains a section to include your Keywords (see Chapter 17). This serves as a reminder of the Keywords that you have decided you will target throughout your content creation process.

The content you produce has two audiences – your readers and Google. Google doesn't care too much about your topic. Rather, they just care if your content matches what other people are searching for. Therefore, your content must be heavily peppered with your chosen Keywords. Your Content Plan also shows you how to do this.

In your Workbooks you will see some sample Content Plans from different industries. You can adapt these plans to suit your own business and industry. Your Content Plan will help you set your guidelines around timing, personality, media and sources.

One of the things that readers comment on in the earliest parts of the book is that all of this 'work' feels a bit intimidating. However, with a Content Plan in hand, they can see that it doesn't require too much time at all. In fact, most of the content production will occur just in the ordinary course of business.

ACTIVITIES

Using your Workbooks you will create your own Content Plan based on our sample plans, you will start with your first videos, blog posts, articles and Facebook posts. This is part of the fun of all of this 'work'. Most people love being able to communicate so readily with the world. For many, the whole process becomes quite addictive. At the very least, it is just satisfying to know that you have the ability to communicate freely, at any given time, at any given location, on the topic of your choice.

You will also be shown how to publish your various pieces across the various media you are using. You will learn how to embed videos into blog posts, you will learn how to set up links promoting your webinars and you will learn how to make all of this available in your weekly emails.

GET THE WORKBOOK NOW

Go to: www.catchupbook.com

Those without the Workbooks can still do all of this work. However, it will just take a little longer to do the research to find out all the 'how-tos'. Your first step is to draft your own content plan using the following headings and the notes above:

Guidelines, Sources, Keywords

The next chapter relates specifically to your website. You will give it a nudge in the right direction to get the conversation happening with your audience …

20

YOUR WEBSITE II

IT'S NOT A BROCHURE, IT'S A CONVERSATION

A blogger is constantly looking over his shoulder, for fear that he is not being followed.

ROBERT BRAULT, POPULAR AMERICAN BLOGGER

A website can't sit still for long without withering. This chapter is all about keeping your site fresh and relevant.

In Chapter 17 you had your website built. But in the same chapter you read that the difference in today's websites and those of a bygone digital era is that our websites change on regular basis. They stay fresh and current with new content being added all the time.

Keeping your website current is essential to retaining the interest of your visitors. If your site becomes neglected it is the equivalent of repeating the same sentence over and over in the same conversation with a person and expecting your listener not to get bored.

The sample layouts that you have used in Chapter 17 will have your blog posts featuring on your home page – front and centre! Therefore, with access to change your blog posts as often as you like, you are simultaneously updating your website / shopfront every time as well – this is good web practice.

In your Content Plan from Chapter 19, you will have some helpful guidelines around content and timing which will probably mean that you need to be producing new blog content at least once a week.

Your Content Plan will also emphasise the importance of openness, disclosure and story-telling in your blog posts. You need to remember that most people favour entertainment over education. However, education is the greatest source of enhanced authority so to disguise the education as entertainment will ensure that you get the readers' attention **and** their loyalty.

Openness and disclosure are common to all healthy relationships. If you're trying to create relationships with your readers (you are) then your material must be a frank account of things. More dirt, less polish.

OK, so you're writing, you're publishing, you're posting videos, you're making noise. But who is listening?

The most exciting part of the whole content creation fury is checking the score. To check the score, of course, we go to your Google Analytics dashboard and you will see a laser-like reading on every aspect of your online success. You will know from one blog post to the next which one is being read the most. You will see from one page to the next which one makes people leave your site more frequently. In short, you will be the ultimate digital fly on the wall. You're even going to see a map overlaid on your site's pages showing where and how often people click.

The point of all of this analysis is so that changes can be made to help you achieve your objectives – more people in your database! So, based on the numbers, you can now go back to your VA / web developer and give them instructions to change and improve your site.

In your Workbook you will see that you can download a Website Review Template. This is a list of questions that will help you to critically evaluate your websites' performance against a set criteria. With the results to hand, you can issue instructions to your VA / web developer and make the required improvements. This is an ongoing process of refinement that all of the best online businesses do as a matter of importance.

Your Workbooks will encourage you to install new content on your site in a systematic fashion, according to your Content Plan

Your Workbooks will also take you through the web analytics process using Google Analytics. You will see a set of criteria that measures your online success and helps you to make sense of all the information that Google Analytics produces.

You can download your Website Review Template and provide instructions to your support team who will implement the changes necessary to get your website pouring more people into your email marketing database.

It's not just your website that needs to be constantly refreshed with new data. All of the other components within this system need new data too. This next chapter shows how to keep everything working well together ...

21

IN ACTION

A STUNNING BUSINESS MODEL, JUST ADD DATA

Happiness does not come from doing easy work but from the afterglow of satisfaction that comes after the achievement of a difficult task that demanded our best.

THEODORE ISAAC RUBIN, PSYCHOLOGIST

Your new business operations model is complete (and it's stunning). You have done some incredible work and this work now allows you to compete more effectively, it allows you to communicate more readily and it puts you ahead of most other people in your field. Well done!

Continuing the theme from the last chapter, we want to make sure that you use the system you have created and get the very best out of it. This chapter will help you do that through the Activities below which serve to ensure that your system is functioning well and is all set up properly.

Some people try to keep a foot in both camps. They will adopt the new system without abandoning their old system. It's important that you use one or the other. Perhaps the most important thing for your team is clarity. Clarity is derived from decisive moves in one specific direction. We encourage you to make it a move forward.

The activities below are simple but important. Enjoy ...

Your Workbook will show you how to complete all of the following steps. For the sake of those not using our Workbook, they are listed here for you:

HIGHRISE

Ensure that Highrise contains all of your contacts within your organisation. Separate spreadsheets and lists of contacts will only derail the adoption process and diminish the returns that you'll get from this new process.

Sync Highrise with MailChimp again. Monitor the culture of your team. Are they using Highrise? Are they recording their conversations? Is there a culture of embrace? Of acceptance? If not, you may need to implement some incentive programs to get people to use the new system.

BASECAMP

Ensure all of your clients' projects are listed on Basecamp with up-to-date information.

Review Chapter 11 if you still need some coaching on how to use Basecamp.

Does everyone in the organisation know how to use it? Is there further training required? For the culture to be healthy around its use, it must be understood. Chapter 11 contains sufficient training material for your whole team to become comfortable with Basecamp.

DROPBOX

Ensure all of your data is available in Dropbox. Just like Highrise, you can't have more than one system. It all must be consistent. The benefit of any system diminishes rapidly when there is confusion over its use.

EMAILS

Review your settings. Do you need new mailboxes for staff? Do you need to allow access to your own mailbox for assistants or others on the team? The Workbook for Chapter 10 will show you how to do all of these things.

WIKI

Make sure that you have a policy that encourages everyone to contribute to your wiki.

Take the lessons from this program and make pages in your wiki that teach these same lessons to your team.

Performing these simple review steps will be a major step forward in the adoption of the system as a whole. This is mainly internally focussed. The next step is to review your strategy on external email communications …

22

JUST PUTTING IT OUT THERE

HOW TO LET EVERYONE KNOW YOUR STORY

We have technology, finally, that for the first time in human history allows people to really maintain rich connections with much larger numbers of people.

PIERRE OMIDYAR, CO-FOUNDER OF EBAY

I have a personal wish. It is that you will continue a constant and vigilant email campaign with your people. I truly believe that this is essential to good commercial communications. This chapter is designed as a prompt to do so and it includes some snappy tips on how to be an effective email marketer.

UNSUBSCRIBES – HOW TO AVOID THEM

The dark side of email marketing. Unsubscribes hurt. I take them quite personally. I wonder for days why someone wouldn't want to hear my careful banter about technology. I'm left feeling abandoned and unwanted. It is not good for my ego.

However, I do know better. I know that unsubscribes are a healthy refining process that actually helps me. It distils my audience down to a group of genuinely interested readers.

Although, there are 3 main mistakes that people can make which lead to unfortunate unsubscribes. These aren't the healthy refiners, they are the casualties of bad emailing practice and they should be avoided at all costs.

SALES WITHOUT VALUE

I learnt a formula for successful email marketing that will always make me welcome in anybody's inbox. It goes like this:

Value - Value - Value - Sell - Value - Value - Value - Sell ...

This means that for each email that attempts to sell something, there must have been at least 3 emails preceding that sales email that delivered genuine value without charge. Only then will the recipient allow you to actively promote something for which you aim to gain a fee. 3:1. That's the rule. And it works. It can be applied to each individual email as well. That is, in a single email, for every article that is promoting something that you are selling, there must be at least 3 other articles that are providing obvious and substantial value surrounding the promotion.

To try to make sales using emails without providing at least 3 times the value is going to get you tossed out along with every other pamphlet that arrives in the mail.

SHOTGUN

To think that because you met that guy at a bar 3 years ago means that he is interested in your legal practice is a stretch and an unwelcome one for him. If he hangs around he is just being courteous and he is falsely inflating your numbers.

Don't make a land grab for people just to get your numbers up. Better to be speaking with 3 people who really care than 3000 who mainly don't. You want fans not flakes.

These unsubscribes will happen quickly and they will be discouraging but these people should never have been on your list in the first place. People should opt-in not just get tossed in. Register first that they have at least a vague interest in your topic, preferably a strong interest. You will get more feedback, comments and kudos when your audience are there because they want to be there.

IRRELEVANCE

One of the important things about the Content Plan is to keep you on track and on song. A lot of people get enchanted by a big list and they start to stray. They often turn the email marketing platform into a personal soapbox from which they may begin to espouse their opinion on all manner of things regardless of how relevant it is to the audience.

Once you have decided your topic, stick to it. Your audience will demand consistency and relevance for them to continue to pay attention.

If you start to deliver content that is no longer relevant to your business and what people expect of you then people will fail to see the value in your content and move to bring it to a close by unsubscribing.

The only time that your content should change is when, by candid feedback, a substantial portion of your audience tells you that they want something different. Until then, there is an implied agreement that you will continue to deliver the same material.

MailChimp is a fantastic tool for email marketing. It contains everything that you need to get started and continue to deliver high quality messages in a professional format. You should now have your email template set up to accommodate your content and your list is now in shape and ready to receive.

If you've not yet sent an email, now is the time to do it. Please revisit the exercises in Chapter 13 for the tips on how to get going.

If you have already commenced, congratulations! I'm sure you're having a blast with all of the feedback you are getting. Isn't it great to be speaking with all those people? You really feel like you are reaching out and making friends, right?

If you haven't sent your first email, now is the time to do it. Your Workbook will show you examples of what your first and ongoing emails should include. From your first introductory email that gets everyone warmed up (not shocked into unsubscribing) to your template that dictates the layout for your ongoing campaigns, this section will help you build a momentum around your communications which will be able to be maintained.

GET THE WORKBOOK NOW

Go to: www.catchupbook.com

In the next chapter, we are going to finally see the sweet rewards of all of our labour – we are going to see what impact all of this has on our bottom line. For this, we refer to our brilliant online accounting resources ...

23

PERFECTING YOUR ACCOUNTING SYSTEM

Balanced budget requirements seem more likely to produce accounting ingenuity than genuinely balanced budgets.

THOMAS SOWELL, ECONOMIST

One of the revolutions that this program brings to you is accounting done better.

Most business people can appreciate the frustration that exists in not only getting information into an accounting system but then also trying to get it out in a meaningful format and in a reasonable time.

Most accounting systems install the accountant as gatekeeper to all financial information by default. Because it's only the accountant that understands how to use the accounting software, it's only he or she that can produce a reliable report.

With the software that we have introduced to you – Xero and Freshbooks – this is no longer the case.

Firstly, a lot of your information finds its way into these programs automatically. This alone saves you hours and hours. These programs will drag information from your bank account and dump it into the right fields, it will drag information from Basecamp and automatically create an invoice for you.

Then, with all of the information in, getting reports is as simple as point-and-click. All the data is online and available wherever you and a computer are.

Whilst you will still need some initial advice from your accountant about how where you should be allocating your expenses for the sake of tax, once your software is set up, you are largely independent and free to come and go from your accounting reports as you please. And, of course, there is no fee associated with you accessing this data when you are capable of doing it yourself.

As a post-installation checklist, the items below are those that should be in place for you to be confident that you accounting system is set up properly:

- A BOOKKEEPER WHO UNDERSTANDS HOW XERO AND FRESHBOOKS
- AN ACCOUNTANT WHO UNDERSTANDS HOW XERO WORKS
- FRESHBOOKS LINKED TO YOUR BASECAMP ACCOUNT
- XERO LINKED TO YOUR FRESHBOOKS ACCOUNT
- IN THE ACTIVITIES BELOW WE SHOW YOU HOW TO CREATE THE FOLLOWING REPORTS ON YOUR NEW SYSTEM
- AN ESTIMATE – AND HOW THESE LOOK TO YOUR CLIENTS
- AN INVOICE – AND FURTHER DETAILS ABOUT HOW THESE WORK
- ACCOUNTS AGEING – HOW MUCH MONEY YOU'RE OWED
- PROFIT & LOSS – HOW MUCH YOU'RE MAKING
- BALANCE SHEET – WHAT YOUR BUSINESS IS WORTH

All of the Activities below go into more detail about how your system works and how to use it. This whole chapter is designed to get you feeling really familiar with the numbers in your business. With a clear understanding of your numbers you can accurately forecast and plan. This is a major advantage for businesses that have Caught Up.

Your Workbook will help you to make sure that you have accounting team that understands your new tools and it will take you through the process for getting the following activities complete:

1. Linking your Freshbooks account to Basecamp
2. Linking Xero linked to your Freshbooks account
3. Adjusting your Xero accounts settings to extract your bank account and Freshbooks data
4. Produce an estimate and understand how these work
5. Produce an invoice and see what they look like from

the clients' perspective

6. Prepare an ageing accounts statement

7. Prepare a P&L

8. Prepare a Balance Sheet

You may not do all of these things at once but the Workbook is there for you for as long as you want. You can keep on referring back to it until you are comfortable with how it is working.

This section can be a little tricky if you don't have access to the Workbook. You should contact us if you require any assistance.

You are now at the end of this section and almost at the end of the book! The last section of the book will set you on a course to continue this good work ...

23

A SCHEDULE FOR DELIVERING CONSISTENCY AND EXCELLENCE

People in their handlings of affairs often fail when they are about to succeed. If one remains as careful at the end as he was at the beginning, there will be no failure.

LAO TZU

Our 2-day journey has just about come to an end. In this last couple of days, you and I have built something truly valuable. You now have the ability to:

- communicate effectively with your audience
- operate your business remotely
- offer an amazing service experience to your clients
- produce meaningful accounting reports instantly
- scale up and down without time lag or infrastructure costs
- extract value from all of your intellectual property
- track your relationships with everyone you do business with

and so much more ...

With this system in place you have achieved something that is unique and progressive but your success with it will be determined by how well you deliver now that you have the ability to. Your clients have the right to expect a lot more from you now. Your partners, staff and suppliers do too. Your choice to adopt and implement this program is ongoing.

In your Workbook there is a timetable that shows when you

need to conduct the activities that will keep this system working in your business. It's important that this work continues to take place in order for your new system to continue to be an integral part of your business.

Also, what you and I have learnt together in the last couple of days is really just the beginning. This work just helped you to Catch Up. The next challenge is in keeping up!

We are committed to you and we want to make sure that your knowledge remains just as current as anyone else's. That commitment ensures that we remain at the forefront of everything new in technology. We study the latest trends and we are part of the ongoing conversation in this field and we update your Workbook every time we come across a new innovation. If you have access to the Workbook, you will automatically get access to the new tutorials on the latest technology available for your business.

GET THE WORKBOOK NOW

Go to: www.catchupbook.com

Thank you for joining me on this 2-day journey. I truly hope that this has made a positive difference in your business. I am grateful for your attention and I hope to keep in touch with you for a long time.

Until we speak again, all the very best

Wayne Butcher and the Catch Up Team

In your Workbook you will see a timetable that sets out the schedule for completing the important tasks that keep your system running. It's important for all the users of your system that you keep it up-to-date.

For those not using the Workbook, there is a summary of the schedule below:

DAILY

- Facebook posts
- Google Analytics – monitor and refine the website

accordingly

- Freshbooks reconciliation – reconcile to bank account deposits daily

WEEKLY

- New blog post
- New video
- Email newsletter to your database
- P&L Statement
- Ageing Accounts Statement

MONTHLY

- Webinar

www.ingramcontent.com/pod-product-compliance
Lightning Source LLC
Chambersburg PA
CBHW071755200526
45167CB00018B/1808